"Lorena Escoto Germán walks us throug[h] [...], wholistic, liberating, and necessary! *Text[...]* [...] [every] teacher should read. Not only does the [...] [meet] students where they are and learning wh[...] [us as educators] to grow and become the teache[rs] [we are meant to be.] Centering education in love, community, justice, truth, and knowledge, Germán pushes us to go beyond ourselves and to be present and to open our hearts to the possibilities of justice-centered learning."

—Tiffany Jewell, author of the #1 *New York Times* best seller, *This Book Is Anti-Racist*

"As this country becomes more divided, this book helps educators step into the liberation work with both feet. Germán has written the teaching book that will hopefully push teachers and their classrooms to more justice-centered practices and orientations."

—José Luis Vilson, Executive Director of #EduColor, NYC math educator, and author of *This Is Not a Test*

"*Textured Teaching* is a combination of affirmation, culturally relevant practices, culturally sustaining teaching, and liberating pedagogies. It is love. It is truth-telling. It is nuanced. It is hopeful. It is necessary in its stance and commitment to dismantle harmful schooling practices through pedagogical restoration, equity, and justice. In fact, it is Lorena Escoto Germán's commitment to anti-oppressive and anti-racist teaching, which is felt on every single page of this book, that should encourage us to reimagine teaching as a Project in Humanization that positions teachers as learning partners alongside students. What a beautiful text. What a layered teaching framework. What a textured book. Read it and be left inspired!"

—Valerie Kinloch, Renée and Richard Goldman Dean & Professor, School of Education, University of Pittsburgh

"The craft of teaching is both science and art, but Textured Teaching suggests that it also wisdom and discovery. The wealth of this approach, subtle in its implication, transformative in its intent, is found at the fertile intersection of where profound education work sits in the lives of youth; to equally empower, enhance, and sustain them while fostering conditions that promise they will grow."

—David E. Kirkland, Executive Director, NYU Metro Center and Professor of Urban Education, New York University

TEXTURED TEACHING

A FRAMEWORK FOR CULTURALLY SUSTAINING PRACTICES

LORENA ESCOTO GERMÁN

HEINEMANN
Portsmouth, NH

Heinemann

145 Maplewood Avenue, Suite 300

Portsmouth, NH 03801

www.heinemann.com

Offices and agents throughout the world

The author and publisher wish to thank those who have generously given permission to reprint borrowed material:

Figures 1–1 and 1–2: Reprinted with permission of Learning for Justice, a project of the Southern Poverty Law Center.

Acknowledgments for borrowed material continue on p. 144.

Library of Congress Cataloging-in-Publication Data
Name: Germán, Lorena Escoto, author.
Title: Textured teaching : a framework for culturally sustaining practices
 / Lorena Escoto Germán.
Identifiers: LCCN 2021018530 | ISBN 9780325120416
Subjects: LCSH: Culturally relevant pedagogy—United States. | Critical
 pedagogy—United States. | Social justice and education—United States.
Classification: LCC LC1099.515.C85 G47 2021 | DDC 370.11/5—dc23
LC record available at https://lccn.loc.gov/2021018530

Editor: Louisa Irele
Production: Victoria Merecki
Cover art: SOFAHOOD
Cover and text designs: Monica Ann Cohen
Author photo: Fresh Creativo Photography
Typesetting: Shawn Girsberger
Manufacturing: Val Cooper

Printed in the United States of America on acid-free paper
2 3 4 5   CGB   25 24 23
PO 4500865199

FOR ANALÍZ, ZION, AND SOL,
AND FOR EVERYONE ELSE'S
CHILDREN WHO ARE BLACK, BROWN,
INDIGENOUS, IMMIGRANT, AND
MORE, WHO HAVE STORIES TO TELL
AND ARE STARDUST, TOO.

CONTENTS

FOREWORD

Imagine what it would be like if that extraordinary social justice educator who has been throwing down beautiful work with communities for years was willing to share all of her brilliance, commitment, heart and soul work with you, one-on-one, with all the receipts, all the reading and research, nothing held back, just the beautiful and honest truth of her practice. That is what *Textured Teaching* is: a guidebook for those of us in the ongoing journey of being and becoming culturally sustaining educators, of teaching and learning with communities to build the world we need. As Lorena Germán writes in the concluding chapter, "I want to hug you with these words: we are in no position to consider ourselves apolitical or neutral members of society. As educators, we are either dismantling the unjust system that is education, or we are complicit in it." Be prepared to be embraced with words, images, stories, examples, experiences, a love for teaching in community with young people toward social and cultural justice.

But let me begin at the beginning. As you will hear in the following pages, I have been learning in community with Lorena for over a decade. Indeed, when I was first writing about Culturally Sustaining Pedagogy (CSP) back in 2011, I was just coming to know Lorena. At the time, I was an early career professor, a former English language arts (ELA) teacher now working with other ELA teachers, and Lorena was an early career ELA teacher just getting grounded in her practice. We were both critical educators of color (me, a Black man born to a White settler mother and a Black Jamaican father; Lorena, a Black Latinx Dominican American woman). And we were both committed to centering our communities through education in a system we knew was in many ways designed to do the opposite. In this way, Lorena has been part of our CSP collective all along, and she has been there as we have kept joining communities, deepening the work, learning what it means to center and sustain young people through teaching and learning.

Over the years, when I wanted to connect with an educator doing the CSP work we need, I always reached out to Lorena, and I always followed her work on social media with the #DisruptTexts squad, with the National Council of Teachers of English, or across the many facets of her practice. To be honest, Lorena is a teacher hero of mine. She is one of those educators that all of us—teachers, students, families, community members (and those that hold multiple roles and memberships)—gravitate toward because of her vision, passion, commitment to lay it all on the line in the project of justice for Black, Indigenous, Latinx, Asian, Pacific Islander (not mutually exclusive) communities across intersections with gender and sexuality, disability, language, class, land, and more.

One of the reasons Lorena has been so inspiring to my own teaching, learning, and theorizing about CSP is because she truly gets what CSP is all about. As she recalls from those early years of our learning together,

> What I learned about CSP has become the foundation of my teaching approach. It is what I stand on, unwaveringly. . . . The verb *sustain* is important to note because it requires a depth not necessitated by, say, *relate* or *connect*. To sustain something means you feed it and nurture it to make sure it's healthy and alive.

Lorena understood this essential foundation of CSP early and kept it as her foundation as she taught, and read, and experienced across these many years. This book brings all of this praxis together, with love and vision. I mention love because in our work with CSP, H. Samy Alim and I have been explicit about the centrality of love in the practice of culturally sustaining education. Knowing the kindred relationship between CSP and Textured Teaching (TT), it will come as no surprise that TT also holds love as a core principle. It will also come as no surprise that central traits of Lorena's TT are being *student driven* and *community centered, interdisciplinary, experiential*, and *flexible*. These are all also fundamental features of settings enacting CSP. What may come as a surprise is the ways Lorena makes all of this both actionable and irresistible for educators looking to join the work as well as those looking to deepen their commitment to CSP and other strength- or asset-based approaches. This is to say, these traits, including the core focus on love, are made concrete through examples of practice; distillations of literature, research, and theory; and the essential practice of calling us in to our own necessary divestments from white supremacy, settler colonialism, and attendant cis-heteropatriarchal, ableist, monolingual logics so central to schooling in the United States and so many nations.

Lorena invites us to journal as we read, learn, bring these lessons into our practice—and she offers prompts, cautions, paths forward for our engagement. Through this beautiful pedagogical authoring, we find ourselves invited to practice alongside her. It is an invitation none of us will want to refuse.

Toward the end of the book, Lorena shares this necessary meditation on the origins of TT:

> A truth about Textured Teaching is that it comes from a place of frustration and pain inside of me: the pain of having been wronged by educational institutions; the frustration of being silenced, ignored, and neglected. These feelings pushed me into knowing I could do better and believing that the classroom could be different.

I am so grateful you and I are holding this book so we can join Lorena and the communities we teach and learn with in building different classrooms; so we can, as Lorena writes, "stop wondering and guessing how social justice is implemented in the classroom." No guesswork needed here, only a willingness to join Lorena in laying it all on the line to center and sustain the young people, families, communities we love.

Django Paris
University of Washington on Coast Salish Lands

ACKNOWLEDGMENTS

This book has been a journey for me and will continue to be. There have been so many people that have been there since day 1, and others that joined at the right time. Thank you, God, for the gifts and for opening the doors; for providing and for protecting. Roberto, you saw a teacher in me before I really saw it myself. You pushed me, you nurtured this fire, you loved me through it, you're my iron, and you continue to be my lover and best friend. Analíz, Zion, and Sol: you are the impetus for this book. Your love, support, hugs, and kisses made this book happen. I want to do my part in making sure school is good for you and to you. I want you to thrive. I want you to love learning. I want you to grow and glow.

Thank you to Ma, Dad, Javier, Ambar, Jorge, and Francesca. You are all brilliant. Each one of you is amazing in your own right and I get to be part of this bright group called family. Ma and Dad, you always believed in me, I know.

Thank you to Django and Rae for the love and mentorship. Your support and ability to see in me what I had yet to see in myself will always remind me of the power of teaching. Thank you to David Kirkland, Damián Baca, Adam Banks, and Maisha Winn for your example, intelligence, and work. You modeled what unapologetic intellect looks like. Thank you to Lou B., Ummi, Rich, and my ABL familia. You helped me find my voice again after my silent period. You opened the early door for this book. Jineyda: your support and honesty are priceless. Your comments on the book's ideas, your tips, and your help in every way kept me going. Eres mi hermana, for sure. Jennifer and Jasiela: your accountability and love goes beyond friendship. Your prayers have definitely sustained me and your loving pressure kept me going more often than not. Julia, I appreciate you deeply. I am so grateful that we are in each other's lives. Watching you grow in this profession and expand into the amazing librarian you are right now was certainly an inspiration to me. Tricia and Kim, I'm grateful for our crew and our work. It has solidified the ideas in this book, and I appreciate your willingness to go on this ride with me. Joseph: your mentorship, love, and support have been essential to me getting this book done and for all the other work, too. And thank you for the snacks, the bacon, the books, and the GIFs. Te aprecio mucho. José: somehow you became a brother and I can't imagine not having you around. You modeled for me what teacher support looks like and how to lift as you climb. I'll always be grateful for that. Tracey Flores: thank you for your dedication to us chicas, to us madres, and for always being a beautiful reminder of what intergenerational, purposeful writing and production is meant for. Es para nuestra liberación.

Queridos abuelos y abuelas: gracias por sus sacrificios. Gracias por demostrarnos lo que es trabajar y dedicarse a mejorar su vida y la de sus hijos. Su ejemplo y su empeño nunca fueron en vano. Este libro es producto de las enseñanzas inculcadas en sus hijos, los cuales me criaron y me guiaron siempre.

Louisa: thank you for pushing me to do this project. I know you think you're an auntie to this project, but really I see you more as a sister to it. You were in it from the beginning, next to me through the doubts and questions and hesitations. The comments section of Google is where I learned to trust you. You'll always be my editor. Thank you.

INTRODUCTION

> **Who do you bring with you when you walk into the room?**
> —Django Paris

Textured

My aunt once pointed out to me how the underside of a woven fabric seems chaotic and messy and doesn't appear to make much sense. The colors are going in all directions and the threads seem to be disorganized. Some might even look loose. You can't really decipher a pattern, and put quite simply, it looks terrible! But on the top is a colorful, purposeful, and beautiful pattern. The colors and threads come together to reveal a message, an artistic impression. There's texture, there's blending, and there's variety. It all comes together to create an impressive organization of shades that complement each other harmoniously. That's one way to think of Textured Teaching: a process that has many parts and elements and can even be considered messy, but on the other side of it is learning, growth, consciousness, beauty, and liberation. It's a very purpose-driven way to teach for what we know is good for the future, for what we know is freedom for all people.

The word *texture* has many definitions. As a noun, it can mean the visual appearance or surface of something—like an oil painting with ridges and curves showing us how the artist used their paintbrush—or a creation made of interwoven elements—like a pattern of musical sounds or the fabric my aunt showed me. As a verb, it is used to explain when we actively give texture to what we've made—like adding a sponge effect to an accent wall. Textured Teaching is all of these things. It is a noun and a verb. It is what we do and how we do it. In *The Latinization of U.S. Schools*, Dr. Jason Irizarry explains that based on large demographic shifts in the United States, "the racial/ethnic and linguistic texture of the United States is changing rapidly" (2011, 3). Our future is textured by incoming languages, blending cultures, welcomed voices, true history, robust art, all of life, warm and tasty food, and more. It is interwoven with so much and if we don't respond to that reality we will, in fact, be leaving our students unprepared to engage in the future through our outdated racist and biased approaches. Textured Teaching is a dynamic, culturally sustaining framework with strategies that aim to engage all learners by welcoming all of who they are to work toward social justice.

My Own Schooling

I attended the public high school in the town where I grew up—the same high school that my aunt and older sister graduated from, where my grandpa once taught, and my mom had been an administrative assistant. As I walked through the front door on the first day of ninth grade, I was so excited about the journey I thought I would have there. I wanted to make a name for myself. I, too, wanted to attend a basketball game and cheer for my friends. I, too, wanted to walk into the building and have friends to say hi to and jokes to make with others. What I didn't know was that our graduation rate was at nearly 50 percent and that a couple of years into my attendance, we would lose our accreditation. The majority of my peers and I were Latinx, yet our teachers and administrators were White, and to say that there was a cultural gap is an understatement. The curriculum I was taught was centered on Whiteness in every sense. The values that were prioritized, the culture that was celebrated, the authors that we read, the general content in my classes were all by and about White people. My experience was like the one described by Dr. Irizarry: "a process whereby [students] were expected to memorize discrete sets of facts that were completely disconnected from the material conditions of their lives" (2011, 10). This was and still is problematic.

Textured Teaching is a dynamic, culturally sustaining framework with strategies that aim to engage all learners by welcoming all of who they are to work toward social justice.

Today, as an educator, I work diligently to make sure that my students have a different experience. All students deserve to be seen and have more than what they're currently getting from school. Specifically, they deserve to get an understanding of the diversity in the world and the richness that it brings. To be able to function in the world outside of the school, they *need* to develop a sense of cultural proficiency and deconstruct the harmful practices our society has socialized us all into. So in my quest to be, quite literally, the type of teacher I never had, I concentrated on developing an engaging, thoughtful, antiracist, and inclusive teaching approach. I began by asking myself these questions:

- What can I do to connect with my students in a way that affirms their culture?
- How can I make sure the content is engaging and relevant to their lives?
- What will I make sure I do consistently to have a positive impact in the classroom and in our school building as I strive for change?
- How can I use this content to help students relate to other cultures as well as the world around them?

It was such a challenge to try and be creative under the pressure of standardized testing dominating our school calendar and the Common Core State Standards dictating curricula. We were told what books we taught and some of our in-class assessments were also designed for us. Thus began my search for moments where I could take creative risks. I needed to be able to do the opposite of what Dr. Irizarry shared schools have always been doing: "victimizing young people by treating them as disposable, unworthy of investment, and incapable of original thought and higher-order thinking" (2011, 10). I knew that experience all too well. I wanted better for my students.

I began by texturizing the one unit I was allowed to develop on my own during the year. I decided to teach the Spike Lee film *Do the Right Thing*. I brought in a guest speaker, used supplementary texts strategically, and created opportunities for flexibility in their assessments and products. The students responded critically and were engaged throughout the entire unit. We were able to have deep, honest, and challenging conversations about our school and community. I wish the whole year could have been that way. I wish I had more choice. I wish my students had more choice. I wish that I could have used this type of learning to do more, to coach them into more skill building. I've since moved to a different school environment, but I share this because this is where Textured Teaching began: in the most oppressive teaching environment I'd ever been in. And I continue to use Textured Teaching to this day. I currently teach at a small independent school in the heart of Austin, Texas. Although I have a predominantly White student body that I work with, there are many students that are a blend of Latinx and White ethnicities, primarily Mexican. The size of the school also definitely plays a role in what I can achieve, academically speaking. Our classes meet two to three times per week for about seventy minutes. That structures my planning and what I set out to do with them, in terms of pacing. Lastly, it's a school community that is very unique in terms of its culture. There is a general openness to antibias and antiracism dialogue and work. My administrators are openly making space for that dialogue and have engaged in the work themselves. Textured Teaching works in this setting, too. The approach I am sharing with all of you is for anyone anywhere.

The Shoulders I Stand On

While teaching at my first high school, I earned my master's degree through a graduate program that impacted me in unexpected ways. Although it was very traditionally Eurocentric and focused on literature written by and about White people, for the most part, there was a growing movement toward change and inclusivity. For the first time, I met academics who were people of color teaching about social justice in education and using pedagogy for liberation. My mind was blown and my hunger was piqued.

I met Dr. Django Paris my first summer. He was working on developing Culturally Sustaining Pedagogy (CSP) and would publish the introductory article the following year. Later, he would coedit the text *Culturally Sustaining Pedagogies: Teaching and Learning for Justice in a Changing World* (2017) with Dr. Samy Alim. His work changed my life. Our talks opened my mind. His words encouraged me in ways that healed the academic trauma I was carrying. I met so many educators of color who influenced me in ways that affirmed my identity and expanded what I believed I could do in the classroom. Similarly, I met Dr. David Kirkland and he, too, left an indelible mark on me as a teacher. His course was fascinating, highly intellectual, and so deep. I had never sat in a class like that in my entire life and I was close to thirty years old. He is also a direct source of motivation for the publication of this book. He told me to do it! I realized the power of teaching and why I was in these shoes. All of those academics of color shifted the way I saw myself. I had never seen us shine so bright. I had never seen us walk with such authority and knowledge and power in a space that constantly questioned us. Representation matters.

What I learned at this institution, both the good and the bad, continues to fuel my practice today. Most significantly, what I learned about CSP has become the foundation of my teaching approach. It is what I stand on, unwaveringly. CSP is a pedagogical stance that aims to rectify the ways that schooling has harmed and vilified communities of color in this country. Dr. Paris was influenced by Dr. Gloria Ladson-Billings' work on Culturally Relevant Pedagogy (1995). Dr. Billings' work provided us with a theory that recognized the value and need for including students' cultural backgrounds, interests, and lived experiences in the curriculum and in the school-wide approach. In 2012, Dr. Paris realized that we had to go further than being relevant to or responsive to young people and build a space to sustain their lifeways and communities. He's since partnered with Dr. Samy Alim and together they are encouraging educators to take this stance to dismantle the harmful practices of schooling in the United States.

Paris and Alim contextualize the history of schooling and its historical purpose in our country as mainly forwarding the assimilationist agenda of the state's violent and White imperial project (2017, 1). They offer CSP, which they've defined as teaching that "seeks to perpetuate and foster—to sustain—linguistic, literate, and cultural pluralism as part of schooling for positive social transformation. CSP positions dynamic cultural dexterity as a necessary good, and sees the outcome of learning as additive rather than subtractive, . . . as critically enriching strengths rather than replacing deficits" (Paris and Alim 2017, 2). A close reading of that definition creates for us an opportunity to think critically about schooling. The verb *sustain* is important to note because it requires a depth not necessitated by, say, *relate* or *connect*. To sustain something means you feed it and nurture it to make sure it's healthy and alive. When I think of the ways that schooling has forced assimilation on groups of people and sought to explicitly cancel the use of non-English languages, making a call for linguistic, literate, and cultural pluralism is humanizing and dope. To assert that education should lead students toward positive social transformation is revolutionary and necessary.

This Book

So much of our current conversation in teaching is about what not to do. It's about what to tear down and what to remove. We talk about not teaching certain topics, not teaching certain books, and all the approaches we should not follow. That is definitely important. This book aims to answer what it is in fact that we should do. I propose that it's teaching in a way that is textured, that is nuanced, and that spends time in the gray space. It offers students skills to navigate society and be solution oriented and problem solvers who are authentic and working toward positive social transformation. Textured Teaching is a framework for teaching and learning about texts, centered in love and social justice. The term *social justice* refers to a redistribution of resources, opportunities, wealth, and power that promotes equity. A teaching approach that strives for social justice, then, is one that openly addresses social injustices and functions in a way that leads students to reimagine an equitable redistribution. Our framework is built upon the values that a Textured Teacher must hold. The strategies we use to bring those values to life are the traits of Textured Teaching. Therefore, a thoughtful and intentional implementation of Textured Teaching leads to social justice work.

Each one of the traits of Textured Teaching fills the pages of the following chapters. In Chapter 1, I walk through important definitions needed for social justice work, and introduce the Textured Teaching framework and the four traits. We need to name systems of oppression and the realities of our socializations. We'll do that together. Chapter 2 aims to help you understand how we should be focusing on students, supporting them, including them, and being driven by them. It will also help you see the power in community, land, and culture. I hope to offer ideas for how to build rapport with students, sustain relationships, and consider the community in which we teach. In Chapter 3, I use sample teaching ideas and examples from my classroom to offer practical strategies for making meaning with your students. Chapter 4 is about making Textured Teaching physical, sensorial, and thus highly engaging and memorable. I share ideas for experiential strategies for comprehension and analysis as well as some cautions about what not to do. In Chapter 5, we will think about ways we can be flexible in our practice. Flexibility is humanizing for both teachers and students, and allows for relationships and empathy to enter the space.

You are invited to journal throughout your reading of this book. I want to push us to reflect on our practices and important changes we may want to make. There are journal prompts throughout the chapters that will hopefully guide your personal growth and critical self-analysis. If you're reading this with a partner or a group, that is fantastic. You can use those prompts to share your reflections with each other, and I hope it brings accountability to your experience. Additionally, Chapters 2 through

5 end with boxes titled "Adding a Layer of Texture" that offer suggestions for taking the work a little deeper. If you're an educator who is established in your social justice work and it's embedded in your pedagogy, one who already incorporates some of the elements of Textured Teaching, then those ideas are for you! I thought of you a lot while I wrote this book. I don't intend to assume I'm the only one who has worked on and developed solutions for doing this work, and I know we can continue to learn from each other and grow. I'm grateful you're here, and I hope these boxes offer you a way to expand your already-strong tool box.

My Hopes for Us

My hopes for Textured Teaching and for this book are big. I have wild dreams of teachers becoming better at working with and for students toward improving our society. I have wild dreams about education helping us as a nation move toward freedom and justice. I believe in our calling and I believe in the task ahead of us. I don't blindly believe that all teachers are already doing wonderful things in schools. We know that's not true. I'm writing this very book because of the lack of this approach in my own schooling! And yet, I believe we want to be better. I'm selfishly in the struggle for educational justice because I need our schools and our country to be better for my own kids and for other kids in my life. I want a country where my son doesn't have to be cautious with the police. I want a country that won't punish my daughters more than their peers because they're Black. I have to believe that this can happen. I believe that Textured Teaching will help us all.

We must teach like our lives depend on it.

My dream is for all of us to be doing this work in our classrooms regardless of our content area. My dream is that we will all be intentionally inclusive and restorative in our pedagogy and that in doing so we'll be teaching in ways that inspire love and justice in our students. They will go on and strive toward equity in their roles in our society and lead the change we need so badly. They are our future and the future is sitting in front of us. We must teach like our lives depend on it.

NAMING IT ALL

> The classroom remains the most radical space of possibility in the academy.
>
> —bell hooks, *Teaching to Transgress*

I believe in Textured Teaching because at the core of it is love. A love that fights for liberation with relentless hope. It is a revolution and la lucha is in my veins. This love can only exist when you are tender, vulnerable, and when you truly see the person in front of you. It requires humanizing our students in a system that seeks to tear them down. Lessons and units and daily activities come and go and can be taught by anyone with the right training. Love, though, is in the spirit. It's an authentic connection specific to the students in front of you. Love is an action and a framework. Martin Luther King Jr. wisely tells us that "Hate cannot drive out hate; only love can do that" (1963). So what is going to set us all free? Love. But not the type that says "be kind" yet doesn't address pain or doesn't dig deep into problems. Not the kind that is concerned about superficial smiles or dances on tables. No. The kind of love that acknowledges the struggle and faces it head on. The kind that gets dirty and peels

How does love come into your practice? In what ways do you practice love in your pedagogy? Ensuring that it's not about saving students or whole communities, how do you give of yourself and still enable students to be empowered and self-sustaining?

layers of trauma and rectifies what is wrong. The kind that fights against oppression and defends and restores the hurt and abused. The type of love that gets up in the morning and vigorously sets off to change the world. Textured Teaching is that kind of love.

Why Do We Need to Take This Approach in the Classroom?

Incidents of hate based on a person's perceived identity have been rising across the country. And schools are not immune to this trend. Learning for Justice, a project of the Southern Poverty Law Center that was founded to prevent the growth of hate, published the "Hate at School" report (2019) demonstrating the critical need for the intentional work we must take on to make schools safer for all students. According to the report, in 2017 there were at least 821 verified hate and bias incidents at schools. That is 821 too many. Of the six categories, 33 percent of educator-reported incidents targeted a student's race or ethnicity, making racism the leading motivation. I know many teachers would say they would address racism if they recognized it in their classroom. To recognize it, we need to know the language that is being used by students and we need to understand the way these dynamics play out. What are students saying to each other? What rhetoric are they using and what values and ideologies are they invoking? Figure 1–1 highlights some of those words reported by Learning for Justice.

WHAT KIDS PERCEIVED TO BE IMMIGRANTS GET TOLD

→ Go back to . . .

→ You're not American.

→ You're not a real American.

→ You need to go home.

→ You don't belong here.

→ You're going to get deported.

→ Your parents will be deported.

→ ICE is coming for you.

→ I'm going to call ICE on you.

→ You legal, bro?

→ I will beat you back to China.

→ If your country didn't want you, why would we?

Reprinted with permission of Learning for Justice, a project of the Southern Poverty Law Center.

Figure 1–1 What Kids Perceived to Be Immigrants Get Told

It's painful to look at the list in Figure 1-1, and I hope it's also a source of motivation. We have work to do. It is also important to note where these incidents are taking place. Figure 1-2 highlights that the highest numbers occur in classrooms and other areas where students are typically unsupervised.

LOCATIONS FOR HATE AND BIAS

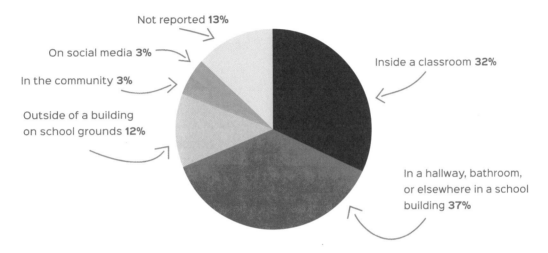

Not reported **13%**

On social media **3%**

In the community **3%**

Outside of a building on school grounds **12%**

Inside a classroom **32%**

In a hallway, bathroom, or elsewhere in a school building **37%**

HIGH SCHOOLS ARE HOTBEDS

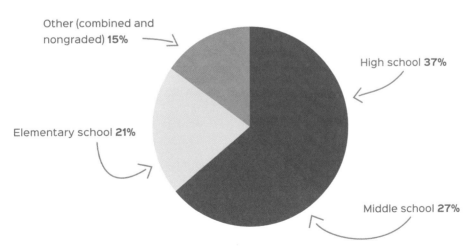

Other (combined and nongraded) **15%**

Elementary school **21%**

High school **37%**

Middle school **27%**

Reprinted with permission of Learning for Justice, a project of the Southern Poverty Law Center.

Figure 1–2 Locations for Hate Incidents

All members of our society can benefit from reading and processing these data. Toward the end of the report, Learning for Justice specifically calls on educators at all levels to begin to identify action steps to turn things around. We need to shift our practices. We must take immediate action to reenvision our classrooms, the messaging in our curricula, and the practices we enact on our students. I offer Textured Teaching as one way to do this work.

What does that mean? What is "The Work"? You may have noticed on social media, mainly, educators and others talking about The Work. Figure 1–3 is a tweet I shared some time ago attempting to explain The Work.

Lorena G. @nenagerman · Jun 12
Do The Work.
The Work= straining yourself to be anti-racist; growing in understanding anti-bias; seek out PD; suggest PD; question, question, question; learn and read and listen and grow; act locally and **strive for change**.

There will always be backlash. Each time. Don't stop.

Figure 1–3 Defining The Work

The Work is an intentional and intense effort to unpack our biases and identify ideologies that have shaped our thinking. All people of all backgrounds have work to do. Although some of us may have to do more than others, none of us are exempt. We all need to do work that depends on truth and justice. It's a matter of life and death for a whole group of us.

Let me tell y'all something: illiteracy is a real thing and its connection to incarceration and premature death is a painful truth. About 85 percent of the young people that interact with the court system are illiterate (Michon 2016). The wonderful and powerful news is that, as English language arts (ELA) teachers, we are uniquely positioned to do something about this—to play a role in breaking down that connection. I've learned that there are several types of literacy, but regardless of the type, literacy is the focus of the ELA classroom. We help students develop prose literacy to read a whole text and extract a meaning, document literacy to search for information in a document and insert what needs to be completed, and quantitative literacy to make computations using numbers and data to draw conclusions. Each one of these forms of literacy has a direct relationship to quality of life. Therefore, classrooms that don't help young people gain these literacies are failing them. There are so many factors for this, I know, and I don't (as I've said before) believe that ELA teachers are the sole contributors to these issues. And yet, we play a role. We are implicated. There are young people in our classrooms that we have labeled disinterested or disengaged. I argue that we have disengaged them; that it is our curriculum that is disengaged, as my mentor Dr. David Kirkland taught me. I say that Textured Teaching is one way to be interested in our students and to engage them. By doing so, and through a more meaningful curriculum, as well as deliberate text selection, we start the work of restoring our communities; of breaking down the connection that leads young people to incarceration. This is how we work toward social justice.

Values of Social Justice Teaching

I often say that, although I believe in sharing resources, I prefer not to share lesson plans. I love to co-teach and I love to collaborate. However, what I teach is because of who I am as a person and the way I teach a lesson is always tailored to who is sitting in front of me. I would be doing everyone a disservice by just giving out lessons that were designed to be led by me and for my students. Instead, I offer Textured Teaching as a dynamic framework with strategies that aim to engage all learners to work toward social justice. Now, let me remind you of what I mean by social justice, because that has become a popular, catchall phrase. I am talking about the redistribution of power and access so that all people, regardless of their identities, have equitable access to resources and power. Equitable is not the same as equal. I'm talking about "antiracist discrimination" as Kendi explains in *How to Be an Antiracist*, which forwards that "to treat some persons equally, we must treat them differently" (2019, 19). This means restructuring how we've historically done things in this country that oppressed and marginalized many people based on various elements of their identity and favored only a narrow few. I'm talking about changing this system so that we can all be free. That is social justice. It's not a topic, a month of study, a unit, a book, or kindness.

Equitable is not the same as equal.

The three values I hold dearly for social justice teaching are love and community, justice, and truth and knowledge. These values lead to spaces where social justice is at the center. Figure 1–4 visualizes this idea through the use of a metaphorical equation.

Figure 1–4 Teaching for Social Justice Equation

Love and Community

To teach for social justice, you have to believe that students are worthy of love and respect; my practices should respect your humanity and by doing so, treat you with love. It goes beyond affection, into action that focuses on sustaining your humanity. We're all part of communities—families, cities, and cultures. Respecting and acknowledging your communities means I welcome all of you and your community's voices. As a Textured Teacher, I therefore value your life and culture.

Justice

In valuing justice, I am concerned with restoration. I want reparations for wrongdoing, equality when applicable, and equity at all times. Justice is concerned with systems that keep people free from oppression via institutionalized harm. As a Textured Teacher, then, your value for justice pushes you to teach in a way where students will question and, ultimately, dismantle the systemic injustices we currently experience. Your teaching is liberating.

Truth and Knowledge

Lastly, to say we value truth and knowledge means we are concerned for an education that is whole, complete, truthful, and fills us with the knowledge we need to bring about the justice we dream of. We are empowered to engage students and each other in learning that is challenging and full of uncomfortable, but necessary, conversations.

Traits of Textured Teaching

Those values inform the traits of Textured Teaching: student driven and community centered, interdisciplinary, experiential, and flexible (see Figure 1-5). These traits are the strategies of Textured Teaching. When strategically implemented, these four traits create an overall classroom experience that reflects the values, is highly rigorous, and is also engaging.

Student-driven and community-centered teaching is focused on people and power. Textured Teaching requires working on developing relationships with students while upholding the value of love and community. In Chapter 2, I'll go into detail on strategies you can use to enact this trait, which involves incorporating student voice, community events, and a general celebration of culture.

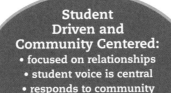

Student Driven and Community Centered:
- focused on relationships
- student voice is central
- responds to community and current events

Flexible:
- welcomes the extracurricular lives of students
- student choice is integral
- diverse range of assessments and tasks

Textured Teaching Traits

Interdisciplinary:
- research based
- requires historical context
- integrates other content areas

Experiential:
- involves using the five senses
- highly engaging
- inclusive literature
- meets different learning needs

Figure 1–5 The Traits of Textured Teaching

Interdisciplinary teaching makes meaning of texts by involving research-based exercises, discussing historical context and making connections, and integrating other content areas into the study of a text to work toward deep analysis. In Chapter 3, I offer strategies for doing this interdisciplinary work, including samples from my own teaching.

Experiential teaching is sensorial and physical because our bodies should be engaged in our learning, both for engagement, but also for comprehension. Using our bodies to learn also helps us to work on empathy because the ideas and content are consumed in visceral ways. Our reactions are honest and felt deeply. In Chapter 4, I spend time talking about how to offer students the opportunity to experience the books you're teaching, how it all connects to deeper learning, and I offer ideas for various books that you can use.

Flexible teaching is one of the areas where we have the chance to enact mercy, grace, and understanding. Being flexible with ourselves, with our students, and with curricula enables us to respond to our students' needs, engage them as individuals, and take into consideration our context. In Chapter 5, I explain how to do this through strategies around assessment, discussion, grading, tasks, and more.

If we think of Textured Teaching as the woven tapestry described in the introduction, then it all comes together when you step back and look at the process of this teaching approach. You plan and focus your units through the framework of love and community, justice, and truth and knowledge. You enact those values through the four traits and develop strategies for working with students. Figure 1–6 shows how it all comes together and is connected. I chose to use concentric circles to highlight how Textured Teaching is not linear, but cyclical. At the core of Textured Teaching is a Culturally Sustaining Pedagogy, and out of that flows the values of social justice teaching, which is the stance of Textured Teaching. In the outermost circle you'll find the traits, or the framework, of this approach, which is what these ideas look like in practice.

Figure 1–6 Textured Teaching Framework and Traits

Bias in Teaching

Whatever we teach and don't teach is influenced by choice, which is predetermined by bias. None of us are neutral when it comes to race, ethnicity, gender, or other factors that compose our identities. Through both explicit words and behaviors of people around us and implicit messaging in literature, media, and other forces of socialization, we are taught to attribute often untrue qualities to identity groups (for example, men are generally more capable than women, Black people tend to be involved in more crimes than White people, or undocumented immigrants—mainly the ones from the Americas—tend to be criminals). These stereotypes, or generalizations seen as a truth, can be problematic because they don't allow for individuals to be perceived as that— individuals—and because they are socially constructed. When these stereotypes have negative associations, then the bias holder has an overwhelmingly negative percep- tion, or bias, about that whole group of people. These biases exist in our minds even if we don't believe them explicitly or would state them as a position (Spectra Diversity 2017; Kirwan Institute for the Study of Race and Ethnicity 2015). Due to confirmation bias, we only see messaging that reaffirms what we already believe, strengthening our biases, particularly when a person is surrounded by others who primarily share the same biases and participate in behaviors that reinforce them. And when they affect how we treat others, they grow from implicit biases into quantifiable discriminations (Collins 2018). Basically, we are socialized to hold preconceptions that are often affirmed by confirmation bias and stereotypes and that can ultimately culminate in discriminatory practices or actions (Figure 1–7) (Kirwan Institute for the Study of Race and Ethnicity 2015). These practices are worse for some groups than others. For example, in a country where the people group is nearly homogeneously White, gender might be the dynamic causing bias and leading to discrimination. In this country, however, White people as a collective group hold the social, political, economic, and general power. Therefore, when they discriminate, it tends to have the largest impact on quality of life and in many cases, life (Harvard T. H. Chan School of Public Health 2018).

Figure 1–7 How Discrimination Happens

This is all very complex. The existence of bias in our lives and bodies is out of our control. Its persistence, however, is not. I don't point this out to make you feel guilty. Feeling guilt is understandable; however, some people's guilt about these biases is unproductive, at best, and at worst, it becomes a tool for manipulation and the reason for their inaction (DiAngelo 2018). As educators, it's crucial for us to understand this and seek ways to improve. We want our students to be engaged in our class dialogue and to be intrinsically motivated to love our lessons. We are constantly, daily, asking our students to learn more, to try harder, to work toward growth. We ask them to revisit their mistakes and aim to do better. We identify their blind spots and help them to persevere in overcoming them. But we all have blind spots. Teachers are not immune to this. This is an area of growth for every single one of us. If channeled into positive action, there is hope instead of guilt. Acknowledging these biases and addressing them through interrogation is much more productive and necessary. We know we all have biases and so beginning to identify and work against them is an important first step of Textured Teaching. How else can we encourage the students in our classes to do this for themselves?

Because Textured Teaching is grounded in a fight for equity and justice, it is important for us as educators to be acutely aware of our positionality in the classroom. Positionality can be defined as the social and political context or reality that shapes your identity. We see ourselves one way, but that may be very different from how students see us. When I'm the only person of color, or the only Latina, or the only immigrant in a room, I'm acutely aware. When I'm not the only one, I'm also acutely aware. Who I am influences what, how, and why I teach. That is the case for all of us, actually. The more we dig into that, the more authentic we can be in our fight for equity.

Racialized Imaginations

In her riveting book *Playing in the Dark* (1992), Toni Morrison outlines the way the literary imagination is clouded by the presence of race and racism. In short, she introduces the idea of an "Africanist presence" that hovers over the writers of American books and is embedded, like a shadow, in the plot and all other literary traits. She argues that there is no way that Blackness is omitted from even the Whitest of books, since it is precisely the absence and distance from that Blackness that creates the Whiteness in the first place. I know: mind blown! And so, in the same way, it is important for us to reckon with the truth that the books we all read in high school, the books all considered canonical and "classical," are saturated with implicit or explicit racism. All of these books are affected by bias. The perception that American literature is unshaped by more than 400 years of Africans on this soil is, in and of itself, racist. Sustaining this myth allows racism to go unquestioned and uninterrupted and maintains the status quo. This idea that literature is "universal" or free from race and neutral is akin to colorblindness and uplifts the status quo, which we know is oppressive. How could such a presence not impact all aspects of life and culture? Of course it has. In her book, *The Dark Fantastic* (2019), Ebony Elizabeth Thomas echoes this by saying:

> Although I grew up in the first generation after the classical phase of the Civil Rights Movement, my literate imagination was quite segregated. Books and movies about children and teens who looked like me were read and viewed out of duty, in order to learn about the past. Books and movies that showcased the pleasures of dreaming, imagination, and escape were stories about people who did not look like me. And yet I was most drawn to those magical stories, for I longed to dream. (17)

We have to interrogate our imaginations and dig deep to challenge these ideas we've learned.

One way to examine the imagination is to study the silence and omissions in stories. What voices are excluded from the literary canon? What stories are missing from our collective cultural knowledge? "[I]n matters of race, silence and evasion have historically ruled literary discourse" (Morrison 1992, 9). The silences have allowed a performative universality to be applied to literature that is insidious. It is toxic. It leads us all to believe that people of color don't matter because we don't exist in the mind or imagination of the authors of our books and textbooks. That is a myth, because of course we do. To exclude us from curriculum is to murder us—to operate as if we don't exist, to remove us from existence in people's minds. In fact, race, the child of racism (as it's referred to by Ta-Nehisi Coates [2015]), was dreamed up by Johann Blumenbach, who decided that Caucasians were in "first place" above other people groups. How we existed in his imagination became our lived reality. It became scientific truth, led to policies, and is life today in the twenty-first century. These subconscious racist imaginations are what lead an officer, an otherwise kind person, to pull the trigger and kill an innocent Black man. These subconscious racist imaginations are what lead people to follow innocent patrons of color in stores due to fears of theft or wrongdoing. These subconscious racist imaginations are what lead editors to think that a Black woman's story won't sell, but accept the same story from a White author. It's these imaginations that inform the books teachers select. And these books build those imaginations. It's a vicious cycle.

One way to examine the imagination is to study the silence and omissions in stories.

Consider engaging with students in an activity around interrogating the imagination. In partners, students respond to a series of reflection prompts:

- Create a list of the voices that are overrepresented in this book.
- Create a list of the cultural points of view overrepresented in this book.
- Create a list of the missing voices in this book.
- Create a list of the missing cultural points of view in this book.
- What social issue or problem is this book speaking to? Is it doing so intentionally?
- What social issue might this book be unintentionally highlighting?

When the partners return to the whole-class group, it is interesting to see what the various partners identified. That diversity of responses alone might be enough to help students see how each of our personal biases informs our lens and allows us to "see" texts differently.

A Radical Teaching Stance

Schooling has a long and painful history in the United States, especially when considering marginalized groups. *Marginalized* refers to people who are left out of dominant culture and pushed to the margins, people who identify as something other than Christian, White, straight, cis-male, able-bodied, and more. For us, our presence and needs are seen as "other." In identifying the original purpose of schooling in the United States, Paris and Alim highlight how the function of schooling was to force upon communities of color a dehumanizing assimilation through a "violent White imperialist project" (2017, 1). Because that is the foundation of schooling, and in many places this is still the underlying purpose of the structures in place, we need to name the injustices and the inequity in our schools and in our curricula. Textured Teaching is calling us to a radical stance: to love.

I've heard questions about why as educators we must take on this fight for justice versus "just teaching" or solely focusing on content, as if there is such a thing. Every single content area is infused with bias and has been used in some way in the fabrication of the oppression of our country. If we all have bias through normal and common socialization, as previously discussed, then why wouldn't the content we have produced harbor it? We would be naive to think that we haven't embedded it in to our educational system. Literature biases were infused and taught explicitly, which dehumanized people of color and marginalized any identity other than the dominant one. Science was used to justify and sustain racism. The project of White supremacy was born in the field of science. Mathematics was used to argue who was and was not a full human. (This is still an issue today regarding Indigenous identity and using DNA to justify someone's heritage.) Geography was birthed as land was stolen and borders, like prisons, were created. History was written by the conquerors, who erased the rest of us. No content area is safe. No teacher is apolitical. If we don't interrogate these histories and work toward teaching holistically, and more importantly, honestly, we are complicit. We are part of the violent White supremacist project and are implicated in the systems of oppression. As members of this racialized society, our imaginations are tainted. Implicit biases are present in our approach to school discipline and dress codes. What we think is possible for some is influenced by what we have seen and been told. What we think is reality is influenced by what has been constructed for us. We continue to infuse it into our students through our current approach to schooling. The very idea of racism stemmed from a person's imagination. In perpetuating these ideas, we are also limiting our students' imagination.

> *Have you ever considered your role in this? If so, how does this make you feel and what actions have you taken to operate outside of this? If not, how do you feel and what does this reveal to you about your praxis?*

In what ways will our teaching influence the imagination of our students? How will we undo their racialized imagination and dismantle what has been constructed? Our imaginations are populated with histories of conquest, rape, theft, power, and dehumanization and its cousins. These antecedents shape how we read characters and how we write ideas. These ideas have been passed down to us from generation to generation. This is especially so when schooling has not offered us a counternarrative— one told from the point of view of the warrior; the ones that fought back. Students as early as preschool are developing racial identities and ideologies. By the time they are in middle school and high school, much socializing and learning needs to be undone. I'm hopeful because Textured Teaching can be one of the tools we use to undo this, to begin to make things right.

Context Is Important

As we work to deconstruct our imaginations, considering our positionality is necessary. This means taking into consideration your political and social influences and how they build your point of view and lead to bias. Our positionality and context are important in terms of how we relate to our students. Who we are and where we are teaching makes a difference and should determine what we teach. Figure 1–8 outlines the more commonly experienced teaching contexts in the United States.

In the first scenario, generally speaking, the White teacher has a heavy load of unlearning to do to effectively reach their students who are Black, Indigenous, and people of color (BIPOC). The teacher is not experiencing the society in the same or similar ways their students are and, as members of the dominant culture, they have many blind spots. Seeing through the lens of the students in front of them requires a lot of self-awareness and consciousness. Due to the systems of oppression that these students have experienced at the hands of White people, there is also a nonacademic learning curve for these teachers and their students to build rapport and trust. As much as the teacher wants to believe they are unbiased and nonracist, the students have to discover that for themselves, which will take time. Acts of solidarity where the teacher speaks up for students, serves them, and makes their trust available and tangible are key. Students have to see that these teachers are not here to be a part of the system that is oppressing them, but that they're willing to take risks and challenge the status quo for them. This work can absolutely be achieved through a Textured Teaching framework.

In the second scenario, the BIPOC teacher often has a positive power dynamic with their BIPOC students and must use that to leverage the learning that happens in that space. In many cases, due to patterns of oppression and segregation in our country, these teachers are either from that very community or a similar one. As a result, for these teachers, trust from their students comes much easier. They can often bypass the learning curve described above for the White teachers. Because the rapport builds quickly and trust happens, sometimes, naturally, the work of Textured Teaching happens seamlessly and goes deeper faster. Often, in these contexts, students of color tend to do better because of the role model effect, which results in

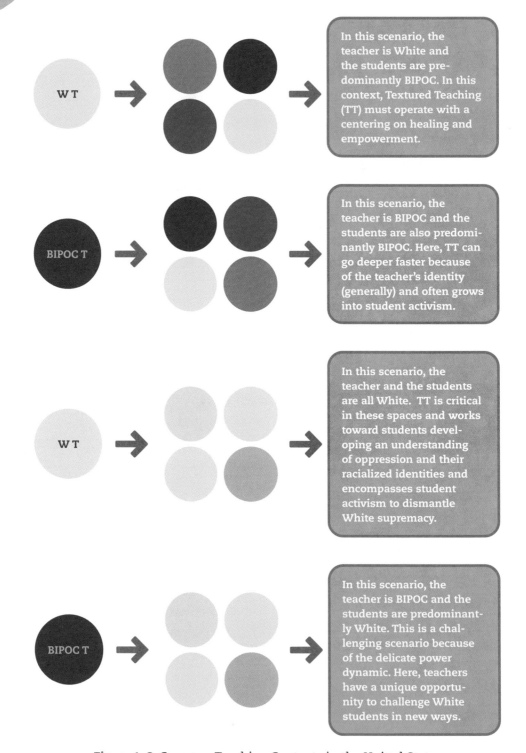

WT

In this scenario, the teacher is White and the students are predominantly BIPOC. In this context, Textured Teaching (TT) must operate with a centering on healing and empowerment.

BIPOC T

In this scenario, the teacher is BIPOC and the students are also predominantly BIPOC. Here, TT can go deeper faster because of the teacher's identity (generally) and often grows into student activism.

WT

In this scenario, the teacher and the students are all White. TT is critical in these spaces and works toward students developing an understanding of oppression and their racialized identities and encompasses student activism to dismantle White supremacy.

BIPOC T

In this scenario, the teacher is BIPOC and the students are predominantly White. This is a challenging scenario because of the delicate power dynamic. Here, teachers have a unique opportunity to challenge White students in new ways.

Figure 1–8 Common Teaching Contexts in the United States

their achieving more and doing better socially and academically (Berg 2019). This is why student activism tends to be more common in these scenarios. Students are more willing to share concerns and these teachers, because they can often relate, create space for that dialogue, and this often leads to strategizing for change. Unfortunately, one negative aspect of this context is teacher burnout. Because of the oppression that exists in these communities, serving students and families through schools can be exhausting. Schools can't solve all of society's issues and that can make the job of the educator burdensome. Students turn to these teachers over other teachers. These teachers, when led by predominantly White leadership, are often overlooked and not supported. Issues develop and the metaphorical cups runneth over, in negative terms. My hope is that this will change sooner rather than later because these teachers deserve it.

In the third scenario, there is a positive power dynamic like the one above it. White teachers are uniquely positioned here to disrupt White solidarity (DiAngelo 2018) and leverage their privilege, so that critical Textured Teaching happens in these spaces. This context, especially, requires administrative support for it to be effective because White parents tend to be highly critical of and involved in teacher curricular implementation. But it's possible to gain parental support. When done appropriately, Textured Teaching is highly engaging for students and, overall, a positive experience. Additionally, these units of study offer White students a new lens for seeing the reality of their lives. They need to see themselves as racialized, as part of the dominant and oppressive group, but be offered hope and ways to resist that perpetuating harm. Racism dehumanizes White people by putting them in positions of dehumanizing others. Offering White students ways to practice love and humanity through revolution is Textured Teaching in action. The teacher can be an excellent model for students for how to act, speak, and fight. They need to see you organizing, pushing against the status quo in strategic and important ways. They need to see this teacher vocalizing their beliefs about oppression, racism, and all the other isms. Centering hope and restoration is an important approach when working in this context.

This last scenario, my current context, is often tense and uncomfortable for teachers. Most common in private/independent schools and suburban or rural schools in predominantly White settings, this context unearths a challenging power dynamic for the BIPOC teacher who is often dealing with White privilege and other social tensions. These are often spaces where White supremacy goes unquestioned and issues of racism are rarely addressed openly. Depending on the school, Textured Teaching can be close to impossible because of pushback and hesitation from students, parents, and/or administration. Sometimes, however, White students are more open and willing to hear about these issues from a BIPOC because of their credibility. In spaces where teachers have curricular autonomy and an authentic voice, this powerful combination can open doors for important work and create a great opportunity for Textured Teaching.

Although Figure 1–8 doesn't encapsulate all of the teaching scenarios that exist or even their complexities, it does present us with the most common ones, considering our country's economic and racial segregation. A Textured Teaching approach can exist in any scenario. Considering your positionality in the classroom can help you identify ways to implement it, how far to push students, and how deep to dig into yourself. Understanding your school is key, because of the history of schooling in the United States.

> *What is your teaching context and what thoughts are you having about implementing Textured Teaching in that space?*

In the end, the work lies in naming systems of oppression, addressing the ways we have internalized them, and pushing back. Textured Teaching requires us to unpack our biases, address them, work on ourselves, then bring that work with tenderness and grace to our students. We become models of the positive social transformation we want them to dream of and work toward. In this way, the work is personal. We grow with our students.

Textured Teaching is complex and it starts with us. Unaddressed trauma begets trauma, and often what we experienced as schooling had major flaws, at best. More often than not, we are perpetuating those flaws and simply handing down pain and structural racism to our students. Once we recognize that education has traditionally been a part of a hate-filled system, we can then begin to acknowledge the need to envision our teaching to dismantle said system. Textured Teaching, at its core, is a fight for social justice, and placing the students and the communities in which they live as a priority is how Textured Teaching begins.

> *In the end, the work lies in naming systems of oppression, addressing the ways we have internalized them, and pushing back.*

Notes

TEXTURED TEACHING IS STUDENT DRIVEN AND COMMUNITY CENTERED

> "When people are oppressed,
> they should resist their oppression . . .
> If we join together in collaborative acts
> of assistance, we can create learning
> environments that work for all of us."
>
> —Jasmine Medina, in *The Latinization of U.S. Schools: Successful Teaching and Learning in Shifting Cultural Contexts* (Irizarry 2011)

The heart of Textured Teaching is a pursuit for justice, and true justice requires strong relationships. So, one of the cornerstones of your practice has to be building authentic relationships with your students and their communities. Students need adults who are caring, are ready to facilitate their learning, and can make way for genuine experiences that prepare them to engage thoughtfully with the world. Right? They need adults who help them help themselves. Students are not in need of saviors, and they don't need any more best friends. Take notice of your students, and allow your practice to be driven by your values, held by their communities.

The Identity Work

There is so much work for us teachers to do on our own, for our students to do, and for all of us to do together. One place to begin this work with students is to engage them in unpacking their own identities. Tiffany Jewell's *This Book Is Anti-Racist* (2020) is an outstanding tool for starting conversations about social justice, race, and understanding systems. Not only is the book gorgeous and therefore visually engaging, it's also a vault of truth and a compass for leading your group to our values of love and community, justice, and truth and knowledge. Each of the twenty chapters offers a succinct lesson for identity building toward an antiracist mind frame. Invite your students to do the self-reflection lessons in Chapters 1 and 2 to develop an understanding of who they are and, more importantly, of how the world sees them, and the lesson in Chapter 7 to make sense of their ancestry and history. By allowing your students to declare their own identities, you are establishing norms of interacting with one another in healthy and respectful ways, and assuring them that your classroom is one for them to be free in. You might discover that your students will want to dive further into the book and go on a journey together to learn more about themselves, each other, and our society. As much as your curriculum allows, let them. The lessons in the book can help you build community in the classroom while also raising awareness of some of the work that needs to be done and the truths our society has hidden.

Your curriculum has to be relevant to, respond to, relate to, and sustain students and families from historically excluded communities. Think about how schools have operated to uplift and execute the project of Whiteness. We don't have the luxury of not working to undo this harm. Our role, as actors in the system of schooling, is clear: we are to heal and bring about change through teaching. So, Textured Teaching brings the community into the class and the class into the community.

The Land Work

The history of the United States is fraught with violence, pain, theft, and blood. In their powerful book, *An Indigenous Peoples' History of the United States for Young People*, Mendoza and Reese explain how "everything in US history is about the land" (Dunbar-Ortiz 2019, 1) and chronicle the injustice suffered by many Indigenous nations. Acknowledging Indigenous People and history is a necessary part of understanding the community of your school. Wherever we may be in the United States, we are on their original land. As you begin to bring community into the class, it's important to be deliberate about not erasing Indigenous People and their history. If you start here, you may uncover what the trauma might be in that community and what work needs to be done. More importantly, you may learn about what students may be walking in with, in their metaphorical emotional backpacks.

To get a sense of how aware your students are, you can begin by asking them if they know the history of the land the school sits on. Some students may be well aware of systems of oppression and wondering what role their school plays in that. Some students may have no clue that they attend school in what is most likely stolen land. What a great opportunity to welcome them into truth! Regardless of your student population, engaging in dialogue about the land on which your school sits begins the process of restoration and connection in that community. Take time to address this and make space for the conversations students may want to engage in, then introduce them to a land acknowledgment.

> Do you know the history of the land that your school is on? What Indigenous People lived there before colonizers broke treaties or manipulated language to take it away? How have you ignored or acknowledged this in your lessons?

In its simplest form, a land acknowledgment is a statement that acknowledges and names the original people of and the Indigenous name for the land on which you are standing. You can also take it a step further and mention the process by which that land was stolen. For example, as I write this, I sit on Tonkawa land. In a blog post on her website (American Indians in Children's Literature), Dr. Debbie Reese offers best practices when doing a land acknowledgment and resources to start your search for information. The key takeaway is to do your research. A good website to start your search is https://native-land.ca. Or, as of this writing, you can text your zip code to (907) 312-5085. But don't worry, you don't have to do any of it alone, you can do it alongside your students! Figure 2–1 lists some questions you can ask to invite students into the conversation with you. Typically, I do this at the start of the school year, but I can see arguments for doing this at the start of a unit focused on Indigenous literature. When done correctly, a land acknowledgment can be a powerful experience that brings a level of awareness and purpose to the work in the classroom moving forward. Everyone in the room is called in to consider the pain of the loss, the resilience of the people who have been erased, the vibrancy of the language, and how to move ahead

- How might Indigenous People have felt when the land was taken away?
- How might Indigenous People feel today about these historical events considering how it has all impacted their present-day life?
- How might we see modern-day versions of what happened then, happening now?
- What is something we can do to support our local nation or tribe?

Figure 2–1 Discussion Questions About Land Acknowledgments

with respect. This statement also sets an important tone: you are striving for social consciousness, you are open to seeing the truth as ugly as it may be, this will be a classroom for restoration, and you are welcoming students into this journey with you, and to do so, honest relationships will be necessary. If students know you value your relationship with them, they'll be able to trust that you are truly trying to develop a classroom where their needs and interests drive curriculum as much as possible—one where you see them as leaders who walk into the room with a wealth of knowledge and literacy practices.

Have you ever done a land acknowledgment? What feelings come up when you consider integrating this into your practice? What things are you excited about? How can you amplify these feelings? What challenges or hesitations come to mind? How can you overcome the challenges?

Community Centered

When you plan a course or select texts or design a unit, do you consider what your students are interested in? What content do they consume in their social and personal lives? What is happening in their local communities? I'm not talking about gimmick bulletin boards with a cool rapper display, or the infamous handshakes at the doorway. Although these things aren't inherently bad, they do not build relationships and create genuine trust. Dr. Gloria Ladson-Billings articulated, "Over and over I see young, White teachers on YouTube doing routines with their urban, mostly Black students to popular songs . . . as proxies for cultural knowledge and competence. Instead of actually reading, observing, and engaging in conversation with people who are a part of a culture they are learning . . . No. Just no" (Paris and Alim 2017, 152). Units focusing on the troubling gentrification

developing down the street? That builds relationships. That builds trust. That dimin-
ishes disconnect and creates teaching centered on love and justice. A community-
centered teacher is aware of what is happening in that local community, values that
land and the justice the community may need to work toward, and incorporates that
community into the classroom curriculum however they can.

Community-driven teaching requires that you consider your positionality, what
community you are teaching in, and how this plays a role in the curriculum. Teachers
who are members of the community they teach within may have the advantage of
insight into the needs and opportunities. But whether you're a local resident or
not, all teachers can read the local newspaper, tune in to the local news, check
in and chat with parents, and create space in the curriculum for students to share
what is happening and their community-centered concerns. As you stay abreast of
the community's struggles, actions, successes, you and your students become researchers, ethnographers, advocates, and writers of community affairs. This is also
an opportunity for you to connect with two important stakeholders of the community: parents and community organizations. I know you already know the importance of developing positive and warm relationships with them, so the real issue at
hand is: How can I build a healthy relationship with parents who seem distant and
disconnected or with overbearing parents who should actually take less space?
I get it. I've dealt with both. The first step is identifying communication methods
that work for each family. It won't be one-size-fits-all, and although it can require
some extra steps that make our jobs harder, it does make a world of a difference. I
send a monthly newsletter to parents (Figure 2–2) that informs them of the topics
we're discussing, the books we might be reading, and the issues that may come
up. Depending on the parents' individual needs and comfort level, I distribute this
newsletter by email, via our school's communication platform, as a text message
link, or as a printed hard copy. To engage students and offset the additional effort, I
get them involved. I have them help to make this happen. They might get the documents from the printer, help come up with some of the content, or remind me when
it's time to send the newsletter. More often than not, conversations from our classes
continue at home. When parents are looped in preemptively, they don't have to ask
their kids, "What did you talk about today?" or "What did you learn?" They already
feel included and can simply join in on the dialogue. Newsletters create a positive

Middle School Social Justice Update

Hello, parents!

I hope you are all doing well. This week's update shares what is going on with MS Social Justice for the next several classes.

Our first unit: Indigenous People and Civil Rights

In small groups, students worked on researching some foundational topics in order to understand issues affecting Indigenous People in what is now the United States. After they researched, they presented and taught their peers. They gathered the information and organized it in a way that would be comprehensible. This week we're doing presentations, I'll be introducing their action project, and next week we will be away on some field trips.

Topics students presented on

Colonization and Columbus

Wars and battles

Treaties, land issues, and reservations

Assimilation schools

Mascots and stereotypes

Follow-up resources

Here's a book you can read and discuss with your student related to this topic:

An Indigenous People's History of the United States for Young People by Roxanne Dunbar-Ortiz, adapted by Debbie Reese and Jean Mendoza (2019)

Figure 2–2 Sample Newsletter

energy between us, even if we don't see each other regularly. This also opens the door for communication from parents so it's two-way and you become knowledgeable about life outside of class.

In addition to staying abreast of what's happening in your community, you can incorporate real-time issues in your curriculum by inviting community organizations and change agents to engage with your students. Additionally, this is an opportunity to offer these organizations access to young people in a safe environment. Often, local organizations host their events in public spaces. Young people may not be able to participate if they can't secure transportation or might not feel welcomed to participate fully if they have to attend with their parents. Bringing the organization to the students eliminates many barriers to access and allows our students to see, firsthand, what advocacy looks like in action and that working for change is possible. A problem-solving classroom prepares students to engage in grassroots efforts that work toward liberation. As you all learn about local issues, you welcome students into the conversation and create curricular space to engage in writing and working on solving issues.

But how do you know which issues students want to address in the classroom? Keep in mind that the topic itself is not the most important part. The real magic is in the process: highlighting for students what they're achieving, showing them how change happens, revealing to them power structures and systems at play in society, and encouraging them to use their voice and skills to take it on. Figure 2–3 offers three ways to select a community issue to take on. The words in bold emphasize who has the choice. In Smash It and Group Topics, students ultimately make the final decision about the issue; in One Problem, the teacher selects for the students. Either way, as much as possible, be sure to maintain student choice in the method you use for addressing the issue once it's chosen. When students take ownership of the process, they become responsible for the outcomes, leading to genuine learning. Although you are facilitating, offering insight, suggesting techniques, and polishing details, they should be driving the process. I go into more detail about this in Chapter 5, "Textured Teaching Is Flexible." We're gonna have to be patient, y'all.

Classroom Community

The students make the class and that class becomes its own community. The physical setup of the classroom communicates who is centered in the class community. There are classrooms that are often clearly designed for the teacher: student movement is structured to occur around the teacher's desk, which takes up a big space in the room, and student desks are set up to focus students' attention on the board or the front of the room. The walls primarily feature teacher-created or store-bought decor. Teacher-centered classrooms make it clear that it is not the students' space. But when the physical classroom space communicates that the room is for students, they feel more comfortable taking ownership over their learning. We can all ask ourselves, how can

NAME	STRATEGY
Smash It	On a piece of paper, students write down what they're most mad at or what bothers them most about their community. When you instruct them, they can collectively express their frustration by crumpling up their paper and throwing it at the board! A couple of students then go and open the papers and jot down all the ideas on the board.
	As a class, you select only one to address together. You may consider specific roles students embody during these whole-class projects to avoid confusion or disengagement. You may also want to consider requiring a reflection toward the end or afterward to offer students space to think through their experience.
Group Topics	With several students taking notes at the board, you facilitate a brainstorming session of all the topics students want to address in their community and categorize them.
	As a class, distill the list to four or five items, and form small groups around those topics. The small work groups will require you to multitask but can be highly engaging for the whole class. Students' voices are heard, they get to address what they want, and many topics are discussed. Your facilitation for each small group plays a large role in their success.
One Problem	**As a teacher, you identify an important issue in the community that you want the class to tackle.** You may choose the issue because you already have resources you can pull for this conversation or you know beforehand that it's pressing and the majority of the group wants to discuss it. Then, use the background-building strategy (in Chapter 3) to help students understand the context and the problem. You can be flexible by allowing them to work on this as a whole class or in small groups.

Figure 2–3 Project Brainstorm Strategies

we to shift away from teacher-centered classrooms and more toward student-driven spaces that make space for Textured Teaching and learning? Figure 2–4 presents questions to guide you as you set up your classroom. I'll explain each question in the following sections.

Classroom Texts and Libraries

The texts present in the classroom and how they are used are an equally important element of the physical space. There are two things to think about when considering texts. The first is the array of the texts themselves, reflecting on how and why we select texts to be in our curriculum and classroom libraries. The second is whether students will get the most out of the text by selecting and reading them independently or through whole-class reading of a text selected by the teacher.

Accessibility and Wall Use

The materials in the classroom should be accessible across various needs. These needs include neurodiversity, or different ways of learning and thinking, as well as languages, tastes, and more. If you want to invite students to collaborate and see the English language arts (ELA) classroom as a reflection of the working world, set up

- What is the main focus of the room, and is it centered on student needs?
- Are the materials in the room accessible to all students?
- What is on the walls? Does it reflect multiculturalism? Does it involve honoring the students in the room, in the community, or missing voices?
- Can the room's setup easily accommodate guest speakers? Movement?
- Have students played a role in the setup?
- Have students contributed to defining and structuring the classroom culture and rules?

Figure 2–4 Classroom Setup Guiding Questions

tables and chairs in a way that promotes group work. If you have individual desks, set them up in groups of four or five. Even better, if you have shared tables, arrange them so students can collaborate but also view you/the board. Be thoughtful about how you decorate or use your wall space. Aim for student work to be on your walls equally if not more than teacher-created or prepared materials. How much of that content is student work? If you use your wall space to display ELA content, be deliberate about being inclusive of marginalized populations. Consider your walls as an additional learning space and use them strategically to support your students. You want to make sure that it's not overstimulating and will not become a distraction, but you can imagine the walls as an extension of your syllabus or their notebook. Figure 2–5 categorizes information to help you think about wall space. The first column offers ideas of what can be up on the wall to support student learning. In this way, the decor is student centered, useful, and not solely centered on your wonderful decoration skills.

Student Needs and Physical Comfort

The setup of the room should reflect student needs and choices, too. Movement is a part of learning, and hopefully, our rooms allow for it. This doesn't mean expensive beanbags or fancy modern chairs for your Instagram account. It means that, if possible, you can move desks and seating around to welcome guest speakers or shift into small groups or partner work. It's important for your room to be easily movable. We

FOR STUDENT LEARNING	ABOUT STUDENT LEARNING	BY STUDENTS
• Terms about literary analysis • Anchor charts explaining key concepts that you will revisit throughout the year • Reading strategies • Grammatical or writing key concepts revisited during writing lessons	• Learning goals for the year or per unit • Antibias/antiracism statements about learning and education • Your values around books, authors, and education	• Creative analyses • Co-constructed definitions • Extracurricular creations • Exemplary work that can serve as a model (being sure to diversify what that looks like)

Figure 2–5 Categorizing Classroom Wall Content

want students to take ownership of protecting that space and cleaning it, yet so many teachers often describe classrooms as "mine" versus "ours," while expecting students to treat those classrooms as "ours."

Cocreating Classroom Culture

So many experienced teachers used to create classroom rules and post them up on the wall even before September started. Many of us do that today, too. In *The Latinization of U.S. Schools*, a student named Ramiro Montañez shared recommendations for adults when building classroom rules and guidelines: Suspending students doesn't work, and "allow students to co-construct the rules and the consequences for breaking them." Students should collaborate with adults to "come up with consequences for breaking rules" (Irizarry 2011, 165). Instead of creating rules *for* our students, I propose that we cocreate these guidelines *with* students. Figures 2–6 and 2–7 are sample guidelines that I cocreated with my sixth-grade students. We use our larger school-wide values and guidelines for our inspiration.

Classroom guidelines are very useful, not just for establishing norms, but for community accountability. In my classroom, we revisit these frequently. We sit in a circle

English Essentials Class Guidelines
Based on PACT and
Community Agreements
PERIOD 2

1. Respect others by listening and being peacemakers.

2. Stay engaged by being present, sharing ideas, asking questions, and making comments.

3. Creatively advocate for ourselves and others.

4. Take restorative care of our classroom and materials by picking up trash.

5. Be a peacemaker during conflicts.

6. Think before you speak, take ownership of what you've done, and apologize when necessary. (Determined by victim(s) and witness(es))

Figure 2–6 Sample Class Guidelines

English Essentials Community Guidelines
Based on PACT and
Community Agreements
PERIOD 3

1. Don't bring others down or make fun of them. Think before you speak and act.

2. Listen with your whole body and participate in all activities.

3. Don't interrupt others. Understand that there's a time for talking and a time for listening. Wait your turn.

4. Don't use bad language or participate in gossip. Remove yourself from those conversations.

Figure 2–7 Sample Class Guidelines

and walk through each guideline and discuss which ones we've been struggling with as a community and what we can do to support each other. It is always so inspiring for me to notice how students are brutally honest with each other, and more importantly, are so ready and willing to be advocates and partners. Students will share which guideline they personally have been struggling with and/or point out a guideline the class has been breaking or not fulfilling. The teacher's role in that dialogue is just to ask questions. You want to make sure to not make judgmental remarks so that this doesn't become about shaming or pushing students into defensiveness. Start the conversation by saying something like:

Do you allow students to cocreate the class guidelines? If yes, how do you do it and what can you improve? How often are they revisited and used? If not, what do you do and how does this approach differ? What would you have to change and how can you do it?

> I want to take some time today to revisit our community guidelines. I want to check in about what is working, what isn't working, and create a space for us to hold each other accountable. I'll read the guidelines one by one and we can share in the whole group what we're thinking and feeling.

Students then jump in and share as the class walks through each guideline. In schools that already place value on students speaking up, being self-advocates, and normalizing "direct communication," these conversations will likely feel quite fluid. In other schools, the conversations might feel awkward and clunky until you and your students have built strong rapport. But it can happen. It requires knowing your students and being yourself with them.

As we walk through and discuss the guidelines, we try our best not to name individuals, but speak in general terms, while using "I statements." It might sound like this:

> I have noticed that I am often interrupted when I speak. I think it's important for people to listen because we need to hear each other's ideas. I know I become frustrated when people interrupt me.

These conversations are a great opportunity for our students to practice direct communication and problem-solving. The skills they gain through these conversations are invaluable, especially in our current social climate. Our students will be able to do things that adults in politics cannot! It will encourage peaceful communication and create the culture you need to engage in those courageous conversations we talked about earlier. These conversations build your classroom culture.

Whole-Class, Small-Group, and Independent Reading

A love of reading will lead students to develop strong literacy, writing, and comprehension skills. It also helps them develop reader identities (National Council of Teachers of English 2019), and that understanding leads them to become lifelong readers and learners. Additionally, independent reading can motivate students to read more (National Council of Teachers of English 2019).

To help students develop a love of reading, I've designed various units where the students selected the texts they wanted to read. Like many of the rest of our decisions, our reading choices are influenced by our biases. To offset this, limit students' choice of independent-reading text to a few individualized suggestions. Research and find texts written by and/or about Black, Indigenous, and people of color in the genre of the student's interest. It takes preparation on the teacher's end, but the results are rewarding and important.

When the goal is to build on students' analysis and literary skills, whole-class novels are usually the more effective approach. In such lessons, representation is how we include communities (and their voices) that education has historically marginalized and excluded through curriculum. I typically select the whole-class novels to ensure Black, Indigenous, and people of color and other marginalized voices are represented. You can still offer controlled choice by providing two to three texts for students to choose between and using a literary circles–type discussion approach where students are grouped based on book choice, for processing and working through those texts. I offer choices, usually, where the books share thematic ideas or specific literary techniques. For example, in one unit students can split into small groups and they choose to read either *The Poet X* (Acevedo 2018) or *Gabi, a Girl in Pieces* (Quintero 2014). Both books center a Latina protagonist, both speak about body issues, sex, power, and culture. Both feature the Spanish language. They're both coming-of-age stories. This way, regardless of the text, students can engage in conversations about some of the same ideas, but they get to choose what they read. We work with young people and that is who we specialize in, not books.

Text Selection

Regardless of how students are reading, teachers should put care into making sure that *what* they are reading comes from a diverse and inclusive selection of texts. Tricia Ebarvia, one of my #DisruptTexts cofounders, published a blog asking teachers to consider various areas where our biases exist and influence our choices. These choices in turn influence the physical space and the learning that happens in our classroom spaces. In regards to curriculum, she asks:

- In what ways is your curriculum shaped by your own educational experiences?
- Whose voices are centered in the texts you teach? Whose voices are marginalized or missing?
- How do you recognize and celebrate the backgrounds of diverse authors already included in your curriculum?
- In what ways do you integrate cultural and racial literacy in your instruction?
- How often do you conduct an audit of your curriculum? In what ways has your curriculum changed to meet the needs of today's students? To what extent do you regularly examine and revise your curriculum to search for problems or gaps? (Ebarvia 2017)

In regard to mentor texts that we use to model writing for students, she asks:

- What writing—and whose voices—do you hold up as mentors of excellent writing and for what purpose?
- What is your definition of good writing? In what ways does that definition include or exclude particular voices or linguistic varieties? (Ebarvia 2017)

Similarly, Julia Torres, another #DisruptTexts cofounder, wrote about her choices to incorporate young adult (YA) books in her Advanced Placement course, but also fights for the inclusion of these texts in curricula in general. She explains, "Reading these texts has allowed my students to access exemplary storytelling, heightened and meticulously crafted authorial style/voice, and socially conscious messages that elevate our students to a higher humanity. Surely, such works are worthy of in-depth academic study" (Torres 2018). That type of intentionality in text selection builds rapport with students and opens the door for relationships. It also serves as a model of what writing can be and that we can all be writers. It's inspiring and motivational.

Remembering that Textured Teaching is dedicated to inspiring a drive for positive social transformation in students, who and what students see through their reading is key. There is much conversation about ensuring that literature and language arts classrooms are inclusive. #WENEEDDIVERSEBOOKS started that conversation nationally, and among publishers. Many authors themselves have talked about it on social media. #DisruptTexts, a movement I cofounded with colleagues Julia E. Torres, Tricia Ebarvia, and Dr. Kim Parker, aims to engage English teachers in that conversation about disrupting the canon and developing a more inclusive curriculum. This is a relevant conversation to Textured Teaching, because you can't see your students' community as powerful and resourceful, but not see their people as such. Regardless of your positionality or ethnic identity in that classroom space, creating an inclusive curriculum is a priority for all of us.

How do you feel about disrupting the canon? How do you feel about the "classics" and replacing any of them with modern texts?

We must be concerned about having texts by women, by people of color, by immigrants, by members of the LGBTQIA+ (lesbian, gay, bisexual, transgender, queer, intersex, asexual, plus) community, and more. They should feature characters that reflect those authors and beyond. These texts should have meaningful stories with asset-based points of view that offer counternarratives to the damage-centered narratives (Tuck 2009) that have created our single stories (Adichie 2009). There should be traditional narratives, graphic novels, books in prose, and others. Disrupting the traditional canon, the one arbitrarily designed and authored by a society that deemed others worthy of colonization and genocide, is necessary. This goes for all teachers in all contexts. All our young people need to see themselves and others in powerful renditions of themselves that offer counternarratives to what our schools have historically taught us.

Remembering that Textured Teaching is dedicated to inspiring a drive for positive social transformation in students, who and what students see through their reading is key.

In particular, YA literature presents a unique opportunity for English teachers. YA literature is an open door for critical thinking and furthers the goal of an interdisciplinary and experiential approach. In *Teaching Culturally Sustaining and Inclusive Young Adult Literature: Critical Perspectives and Conversations*, R. Joseph Rodriguez (2019) explains the three characteristics of YA, which I connect to the core of the work Textured Teaching aims to achieve. He explains that through YA, teachers can offer a counternarrative to the stereotypical models generally offered through the "classics." Through these novels, teachers can create a rich cultural literacy for students that exposes them to cultures and ways of being different from their own. For marginalized students, YA affirms their experiences and identities in ways that offer healing. Lastly, he writes that through YA, English teachers inspire a sense of self and social responsibility because many YA authors are concerned with this and their stories reflect scenarios that awaken these feelings in young people. In other words, diversifying and building an inclusive library and curriculum creates a sense of texture, if you will, for students to see beyond themselves and use literature as a window, mirror, or sliding glass door (Sims Bishop 1990). That texture also works to engage young people and begins to remedy the issue of a disengaged curriculum, which too often leads to what we consider to be misbehaviors.

Although there are many strong approaches and ideas that can certainly help many situations, I'm a strong believer that a thorough and rigorous curriculum paired with an antibias and antiracist teacher can make some important gains.

Culture and Behavior Work

Many educators talk about classroom management and the strategies to implement those tricks effectively. Although there are many strong approaches and ideas that can certainly help many situations, I'm a strong believer that a thorough and rigorous curriculum paired with an antibias and antiracist teacher can make some important gains. When your curriculum sees students, welcomes them, engages them, and is relevant to their lives, then they'll know they mattered to you. And when students realize this, you may find that students who are highly challenging for other teachers are mild mannered, calm, engaged, and understanding in your environment. This isn't about being the favorite teacher or being in competition with your colleagues. This is about trusting that a well-practiced Textured Teaching approach will solve some student behavior issues. It doesn't solve conflicts at home. It's not a solution to all of our country's problems. It's not a checkbox fix-it-all. It is a way to teach that invites students to think deeply and thoughtfully so that there is hope in the midst of social injustice. Engaging in these conversations that other teachers may shy away from is one immediate way to build relationships with students. Dr. Gloria Ladson-Billings explains, "These more politically volatile topics are ones that teachers may want to hold at arm's length. But failure to engage them is exactly why students do not trust schools to be places that deal honestly and forthrightly with the issues of their lives" (Paris and Alim 2017, 146). Unfortunately, there are toxic ways of introducing and hosting these conversations in classrooms, so it's important to keep in mind that bringing them in is step one, but how the conversation is handled can either lead students to feel honored and heard or dismissed and used. That is why as a Textured Teacher it is critical to know and understand how the traits of White supremacist culture live in us (Okun n.d.). It's important to name it all, identify it, and dismantle it, as discussed in Chapter 1.

White Supremacy Culture

The traits of White supremacy culture might seem ambiguous and difficult to pinpoint. They are so embedded and normalized in the culture of the United States that they might not seem racialized at first. However, Dr. Tema Okun and others have identified thirteen traits: perfectionism, sense of urgency, defensiveness, quantity over quality, worship of the written word, paternalism, either/or thinking, power hoarding, fear of open conflict, individualism, progress as bigger/more, objectivity, and the right to comfort (Okun n.d.). In education, we can use those ideas as a framework with which to evaluate our schools and classroom practices. Think about other cultures that you belong to or know of. How do these traits show up in those cultures? In my own Dominican culture, these were not harmoniously present as they are in the United States; in fact, elements of Dominican culture sharply contrast with these traits. When we

> *What thoughts are you having about Okun's work? Can you identify some ways these values may be present in your teaching? What impact might all of this have on students?*

assume one culture as the default, it invalidates other cultures. And, even worse, often normalizes cultures of harm.

Some of the traits of White supremacy culture—including perfectionism, worship of the written word, either/or thinking, and fear of open conflict—are evident in school culture. As educators, we must consider them. Those traits are often present in the ways we think about classroom management and student behavior.

Perfectionism

We often demand perfection from students both in what they produce academically and how they behave in the classroom. Many teachers talk about mistakes as healthy opportunities for learning and how an F is a great lesson in trying again. But even how students fail, how they take the F, how they deal with the mistake has to fall in line with "the right way," "the perfect way." If they have a meltdown and struggle emotionally with this reality, that may often also bring more conflict for them with their teacher. Therefore, our sense and demand of perfectionism is crippling our students and certainly playing a role in the culture we are building.

Worship of the Written Word

The worship of the written word is another element of White supremacy culture alive and well in ELA classrooms. This is why Textured Teaching challenges us to welcome all types of text, all types of voices, and all forms of expression into the classroom. Often, if the curriculum doesn't reflect students or their lives, they don't feel seen or welcomed. If they're not welcomed, why engage? If they don't engage, that will bring negative attention and bad grades. That creates a cycle involving disciplinary measures. There are also classrooms where writing and "data" are worshipped in the sense that if it's not written and it doesn't count toward something measurable, it isn't of value. This is problematic because there are many moments of learning where writing is not the vehicle by which it happens. There are ELA classrooms where discussions don't count toward grades or aren't valued as learning! There are actually ELA classrooms where if students don't write every single thing down, then nothing counts and they may as well have been absent. This sends the message that their presence means little. We cannot continue doing this to students. We cannot continue building classroom communities where they don't matter. Additionally, if you consider Indigenous communities, where the language has no written form or it isn't the primary format of communication, how can you include it in your curriculum to learn from these wise and valuable people if your approach only focuses on written language? We have so much shifting to do. So much unlearning and learning! It's an opportunity.

Either/Or Thinking

Either/or thinking refers to binary thoughts about good and bad, success and failure, and so on. We see this in behavioral expectations where students aren't offered opportunities to make amends and are simply discarded to the administrator's office. This is reminiscent of the criminal (in)justice system where people are discarded by society for their one mistake and thrown away in prisons. In the same way, when there are no opportunities for "gray" behavior, meaning behavior that contextually is problematic but can be managed and solved in the classroom in a way that restores the community, students internalize that binary. What stops a student from continuing to misbehave if they're aware that they're already deemed "bad"?

Fear of Open Conflict

As a Textured Teacher, when you welcome challenging conversations and commit to doing antibiased work with students, you are creating an alternative to the fear of open conflict. No one wants violence or physical altercations in their classrooms. There are certainly limits and safety is important. However, even debates or conversations that can become heated are often avoided due to this fear and apprehension of difficulty and tension. This is problematic because then conversations that can potentially bring healing and teach students how to deal with conflict are absent from the classroom. We are called to welcome that tension into ELA classrooms. As teachers and adults, we can model what it looks like to be comfortable with discomfort. How will our students deal with that in the world? How will they practice expressing their frustrations? How can we teach them in a way where they learn to practice peace? Using Textured Teaching to confront the fear of open conflict is one way.

Textured Teaching aims to de-center those values and celebrate other ways of being. This is a great opportunity for you to model for students alternatives to what we live in today. Offering students opportunities to have a positive relationship with you, as the teacher, across a power dynamic is a great example of how to have a positive relationship with their employers or other leaders. Offering students the chance to engage in heated dialogue regarding topics and issues they're passionate about is how we will one day change this country. Offering students ways to express themselves in a manner that doesn't erase other ways of expression by elevating the elitism of the written word is necessary. For these reasons, and simply because a Textured Teaching classroom is fun, student misbehavior is often minimal and easily managed. The relationships built can endure storms and seasons.

De-Centering Ourselves

De-centering ourselves as teachers is one of the biggest challenges we face. It can happen in layers. This is one of the toughest elements of Textured Teaching. It took me a long time to fully peel myself away. Maybe it was my expectation of control or my need for perfection. I also struggled (if I'm fully honest) due to an age complex I had. For many years I was always the youngest at school and by default in my social life. It created an insecurity in me because I was never old enough, never knew enough, always questioned, and so on. So, when I became a teacher, I felt like I couldn't let my inexperience and age be brought to light. I'd been mistreated, even by colleagues, because I seemed younger than I was. So, I had always equated inexperience or youth with mistreatment. I was afraid and therefore protective. Eventually, after a lot of processing and work within myself, I developed a clear and strong sense of self. I was more confident in my abilities. I trusted my wisdom and instincts. I was like: I got this! Once I learned how to step back when selecting texts, I moved into assessments. Once I de-centered myself (and fears) from assessments, I did it through rubrics. Once students had more rubric creation license, I did it in the physical classroom space. I ended up with a tiny desk on the side of the room, completely out of the way. Think about Textured Teaching as driven by your students, centered on their community, and focused on developing critical thinkers leaning into social justice. To do all of this well and holistically, you gotta be interdisciplinary with it, too.

> *Does this describe your current approach? If so, how can it improve or go deeper? If not, what changes do you need to make to de-center yourself and become student driven and community centered?*

CAUTIONS AND CHALLENGES

Challenge:
You are struggling to gain student trust and rapport.

This is tricky. There could be so many reasons why this is happening. I would start with introspection. Maybe you haven't shared enough of yourself. Maybe you haven't made deliberate space for rapport building and have focused solely on teaching content. When we do that, we forget that we, in fact, don't teach content. We teach students. You might go online and look up group activities that you can do alongside students to develop some memories and moments for sharing.

Challenge:
You're in a predominantly White school/community and no problems seem to be occurring.

That's often a thing: White folks believe their communities are "conflict-free" and "not as bad" as "those communities." Whew! Dig into those silences. Identify who is missing from that school, from that community, and place a microscope on it. Why are there no (or minimal) people of color there? Was that community at some point predominantly people of color? Where are they now, and how did that happen? What does the community do through policies and systems to keep it as it is? Help students see that the absence of people of color is in and of itself the first and major problem in that community.

Adding A Layer of Texture

After engaging in research, identify the local Indigenous tribe native to your region. Consider reaching out to them and inviting them at the start of the school year to lead the land acknowledgment. If you are unable to host a guest speaker, then another idea might be for you or your students to read aloud statements they've published related to their identity and experience. Many of these local tribes have websites where they share important information about themselves. Additionally, there may be a film you could introduce students to that speaks to that particular tribe's story. You could show a clip as part of introducing them to the tribe. The goal of this activity should be to intentionally bring in those voices and accentuate the purpose and depth of the land acknowledgment. A resource that can help with this activity is *An Indigenous Peoples' History of the United States* by Roxanne Dunbar-Ortiz (2015). Although all readers are welcomed to learn from this text, it is designed for adults. You might consider instead using the version of the text adapted for young readers by Jean Mendoza and Debbie Reese, *An Indigenous Peoples' History of the United States for Young People* (Dunbar-Ortiz 2019).

Notes

TEXTURED TEACHING
IS INTER-
DISCIPLINARY

> ❝ Life is not what you alone make it.
> Life is the input of everyone who
> touched your life and every
> experience that entered it.
> We are all part
> of one another.
>
> —Yuri Kochiyama, *Passing It On* ❞

We don't typically spend days immersed in a one-subject-only life. We count items at the grocery store, use literacy skills while reading labels, and practice chemistry while considering recipes. I say this to deconstruct the idea that an interdisciplinary approach in a literature class is far-fetched. An interdisciplinary style is necessary to support our young people to join the world as active participants working toward positive social transformation. It's also one of the best ways to make meaning of texts and fully appreciate the depth of a writing. Think of the skills we use while teaching. We tap into so many parts of ourselves and our lives. We need to find a way to set our students up to be able to do that seamlessly.

An interdisciplinary approach requires bringing together different branches of knowledge, or in our case, bringing together different content areas as we dive into a text and unit of study. Complex ideas can be better understood when we explore them from different angles. When we analyze big ideas and break them down into smaller ones, we can help students understand it all better. For example, U.S.-based racism is a complex social issue in the fabric of this nation, right? It's present throughout history and is at the core of all the institutions in this country. One tool that can help us understand how it all began is the *New York Times Magazine's* "1619 Project" (2019). The strength of this work is the interdisciplinary exploration of how racism is at the foundation of this nation. In it, creator Nikole Hannah-Jones blends essays, photography, poetry, history, architecture, urban planning maps, social studies, music, and a podcast that all address this nation's historical entanglement with slavery. By listening, reading, and consuming the imagery, readers/listeners/viewers can come to gain a comprehensive understanding of racism and slavery. Hannah-Jones earned a Pulitzer prize for her essay in this project. Imagine our students putting together a work like this one. We can prepare our young people to do this. It necessitates an interdisciplinary teaching method.

Complex ideas can be better understood when we explore them from different angles.

Interdisciplinary teaching for a Textured Teacher is approached in three steps (shown in Figure 3–1): demystify and destigmatize, background and research, and supplements and critical thinking. As you read through the steps, think about how you may need to adjust to fit your school's schedule and your students' agility. The suggestions in the table are based on my current school's block schedule (our courses meet for seventy minutes, three times a week). Your time frame or practices might be different, but the goals stay the same. Focus on achieving the goals in a way that works for your students.

Demystify and Destigmatize

When starting a new unit, the first day or so should be spent demystifying and destigmatizing the topics you are about to dig into with students. Often these are concepts or terms that create discomfort, that have heavy connotations, and whose presence causes apprehension for students. Many students (and adults), particularly White ones, hesitate when these topics arise because they are afraid of saying the wrong thing or sounding bigoted. This is an understandable fear: not wanting to say something with an undertone that reveals a bias or hurts someone else. These moments of

STEP	GOALS	METHOD	BEST PRACTICES
Step 1 Demystify and Destigmatize	▌ Define "controversial" terms to be explored in the unit. ▌ Create clarity around misconceptions that may surface. ▌ Establish peace and structure to engage in discomfort.	Whole-class discussion and note-taking that builds community and offers space for dialogue	Display the terms on a screen so that students can take notes in a section of their notebook dedicated to these terms. Look deeply into meanings. At the end of a semester or year, reflect and have conversations that integrate all of the terms and concepts.
Step 2 Background Building and Research	▌ Research events and milestones that may have impacted the author and their writing. ▌ Consider the political context in which the book was published. ▌ Understand racial, economic, and other contexts for comprehension.	Small-group work that is concentrated and delegated	Students make connections to important social events of the time period by considering elements of society that speak to social (in)justice. The teacher serves as the facilitator or guide of discussions and provides students with resources to jump-start their learning, which students continue using computers.
Step 3 Supplement and Think Critically	▌ Laser in on one rarely discussed or commonly underrated element of the unit and highlight its connection to equity and justice. ▌ Facilitate a moment of experiential learning that will bring the study to life. ▌ Consider a lesser known or unique angle on the text(s) and dive deeply.	Partner or small-group discussions and writing	Guided questions can be used to prompt conversation that is conducted through a (Read) Think, Pair, Share process (see page 99). Teacher confers with groups to assess comprehension and make sure ideas are clear. Students' answers can be used as a formative assessment.

Figure 3–1 Textured Teaching Interdisciplinary Structure

discomfort can be used as teachable moments. Additionally, I've come to learn that many of us use these terms but don't always mean the same thing and we're not always clear on what they actually mean. Knowing what terms mean and how to express ideas thoughtfully is an important step to creating more conversation. Demystifying words and destigmatizing ideas are key to creating an environment where people feel they can be courageous.

Consider, for example, a discussion in an ethnically diverse class of juniors. Some of these students had been friends since middle school, so the energy in the room during that class was always open and upbeat. They were always talkative and the lovebirds in the back of the room kept folks chatting, too. But as soon as I projected a slide titled "The N-Word," the class quieted down and the tension suffocated the room. I instructed students to form a semicircle facing the projector screen. I then moved the presentation to the second slide, which had several nervous GIFs and wide-eyed emojis with the question: "What makes us so tense when it comes to this word?" (Figure 3–2). I thought my images would break the ice with some laughter. Nope! So, I nervously laughed and shared what I thought made people stiff. Then one student followed me, saying something along the lines of, "Yeah. This conversation makes me nervous." And the rest followed. By opening up about our individual discomforts and fears, we ended up building a little bit of additional trust within our classroom community. Two important points to keep in mind here are, first, that this type of lesson or conversation is not one to be had in September, at the start of the school year. It requires rapport between the teacher and class as well as trust among students. Second, it's important to build community as a class through the various activities and steps outlined in the previous chapter.

Figure 3–2 N-Word Slide

After this initial conversation, we watched videos and read quick article excerpts to break down the history of the N-word, including its purpose, connotation, and impact (Figure 3–3). It was only then that we could move forward and engage in conversation about such a heavy word with deep meaning to analyze the core text we were studying.

SOURCE/TITLE	FORMAT	PURPOSE
CNN Tonight segment featuring Marc Lamont Hill (2015)	Video	Use this video to hear a debate on the word's use.
Ta-Nehisi Coates lecture excerpt (Coates 2017)	Video	This video offers an interesting viewpoint on its usage.
"Straight Talk About the N-Word" (Price 2011)	Written interview	Professor of the first-ever college-level class is interviewed on the N-word's insight.
"If You Truly Knew What the N-Word Meant to Our Ancestors, You'd NEVER Use It" (Starkey 2017)	Written article	Black man offers his opinion on the history of the word and the connection to its present-day use.

Figure 3–3 Sources for N-Word Discussion

I encourage you to begin the demystify and destigmatize process by identifying topics and words you know will come up in the text(s) and cause discomfort for students. These are often terms considered taboo, political, or controversial, like *race*, *prejudice*, or *queer* (see Figure 3-4 for an example). People may think about these topics frequently, but only explicitly discuss them in spaces where they feel safe or comfortable. Start by identifying words that make you uncomfortable, and as you get to know your students and content, you may find yourself adding to or removing things from your list. It's best to start with a short, manageable list—five to ten words— so the conversation doesn't feel overwhelming. Until your students build the stamina, limit this step to just one class period. As these conversations become more and more normalized in your classroom culture, you may eventually take as many as three classes for this discussion.

When it comes time to work through the list with students, display the terms and concepts on the board—either all at once or one at a time (to keep students focused). Allow students to look at the word in silence for a few minutes—yes, minutes; I've given up to three full minutes. Then, initiate a whole-class discussion either by asking students to share feelings about what's on the board or by jumping right into an open-ended class discussion. Of course, how you manage the discussion depends on many factors (Does your course meet right after lunch when students may be tired or in the morning when they may have a burst of energy to fully engage? Is the list of terms short enough to work through in one session or will it require two class periods? Have students discussed topics like this before? etc.) but the goal remains to develop a shared definition of terms in a way that builds community and offers space for dialogue. The first time you do this with a group, it may be helpful to remind students of the community guidelines you created (see Chapter 2). Each time you have this discussion, the process becomes smoother and smoother as students understand and feel secure within the culture. Even so, it may be helpful to make sure the norms are posted somewhere visible as a reminder to all community members.

After students have aired how the words make them feel, shift the conversation to what the words mean, paying

---

Key Terms for Understanding

Racism:
a **belief** that race is the primary determinant of human traits and capacities and that racial differences produce an inherent superiority of a particular race. It requires institutional/systemic power

Stereotypes:
to believe unfairly that **all** people or things with a particular characteristic are the **same**

Prejudice:
an unfair **feeling of dislike** for a person or group because of race, sex, religion, etc.

a feeling of like or dislike for someone or something especially when it is not reasonable or logical

Discrimination:
the **practice** of unfairly treating a person or group of people differently from other people or groups of people

Microaggressions:
the **everyday** verbal, nonverbal; and environmental slights, snubs, or insults, whether intentional or unintentional, that communicate hostile, derogatory, or negative messages to target persons based solely upon their marginalized group membership

Figure 3–4 Sample List of Terms for *American Born Chinese* (Yang 2006)

special attention to the difference between denotation and connotation. Invite a couple of students to look up the literal dictionary definition (denotation) while the rest of the students write their social understanding of the word (connotation). When those are both up on the board, talk about their differences, similarities, and impact. For example, when my seniors considered the word *bitch*, they knew both denotation and connotation, but it engendered a very interesting conversation about linguistics, rhetoric, and the history of words. They asked questions such as, How does a word develop a connotation? How do we, as a society, decide words are offensive? Can a word ever lose its offensiveness and become "good" again? Students always have so many more questions than they thought they did at the start. They always have anecdotes to share and specific scenarios to run by me. I take this time to answer general questions about the topics presented, and we take on these difficult conversations often withheld by teachers. Time-pressed teachers can consider creative ways to grant students the space to ask the questions they have, like exit slips, dialectical journals, or a class blog.

It's important for students to understand that words have power. Such an exercise allows students to criticize the dictionary as omniscient and co-construct meaning. You'll become wordsmiths and definition builders seeking truth and accuracy. This also allows you to develop nuanced understandings about language and social impact. Additionally, students develop skills around reading dictionaries, searching in the dictionary, and vocabulary building.

To close the discussion, have students write the terms and their definitions in a dedicated section of their notebook. They are able to access these definitions later when it's time to get into discussion for the book, but they can also turn to them for their essays. At the end of a semester or year, you can reflect and have conversations that integrate all of the terms and concepts. In the end, this is about tailoring your lessons for the people sitting in front of you. You can do this. We must do this.

Discussions and Conversations

To go smoothly, difficult conversations need to be approached with structure and intentionality. There are many resources that can be found online or in bookstores, but there are three in particular that I have found most useful. With middle school students, I use various strategies from Learning for Justice's resource "Let's Talk! Discussing

Race, Racism, and Other Difficult Topics with Students" (Learning for Justice 2017). When working with high schoolers, I use *Courageous Conversations About Race* protocols (Singleton 2014). Regardless of the age of my students, I always make it clear that I'm not necessarily concerned with creating a "safe" space. As Matthew R. Kay explains in *Not Light, but Fire: How to Lead Meaningful Race Conversations in the Classroom* (2018), the definition of *safe* varies from teacher to teacher, which leaves it up to students to "decipher what a teacher means when they claim 'safe space'" (16).

What has a safe space looked like in your classroom? What are the protocols? What works well? What could you do better?

In my experience, I have found that often those safe spaces exist to accommodate White people's sense of discomfort in a way that does not get all of us further along in the direction of problem-solving. Kay proposes that spaces where discussions flourish require a culture of listening. Therefore, I'm much more concerned with making sure that students feel supported to take risks, listened to so that they in turn will listen, and courageous to ask tough questions and challenge each other.

Background Building and Research

When teachers talk about background building, it's often focused on vocabulary terms and setting. They define words that students may not know, explore elements of the setting that may be foreign to students, explain any nonfictional characters or events that are featured in the text, and then start the reading. Although this isn't wrong, I want to push us to go deeper with what background building can be.

In the background building and research stage, students develop an important sociopolitical understanding needed to grasp the complexity of the texts we read. Background building deconstructs the idea that authors are unbiased or somehow disconnected from their surroundings, living in silos. That is a myth. Whatever we write, be it fiction or nonfiction, carries us in it. Our souls are in there. Our hearts are written. Our biases are embedded. As we research, we learn details that allow us to identify the examples of bias embedded in texts, and this helps students to find deeper literary analysis of an author's choices and craft. It helps students capture the richness of literature and develop a critical eye and through the process students become historians and make connections across all types of texts and content areas. The process has four steps: the teacher determines the concepts students will need to know, students join small groups, they research, and then they present/teach.

Teacher as Guide

Your role as a guide is specific: suggest questions for research and offer key search words. See Figure 3–5 for the list of topics I use when reading *American Born Chinese* (Yang 2006). The topics span a range of time periods and events. This is also the order in which students present the content. If you read Yang's book, you'll also notice that "Japanese internment camps" is not directly related to the text. A range of topics builds a foundation for students to study this book and analyze it both from a literary perspective and from a sociopolitical one. The addition of Japanese internment camps exposes them to an issue that is rarely taught in our schools and social studies curriculum. You can use this opportunity to welcome the dialogue and help students see how anti-immigrant sentiment and anti-Asian racism do not apply only to the Chinese. It is systemic.

Often, these are topics students are not very familiar with and strong emotions may arise. These emotions are understandable and you should welcome them in your classroom. We feel, we hurt, and sometimes we cry. It's all a necessary part of dismantling oppression. Often those conversations aren't very formal. They bubble up for students as they are finishing their research, putting together their presentation, or having a small-group conversation. Allowing the class to digress a bit is a way to make time for processing this information. Since our ultimate goal is for students to learn and internalize this work, making space for them to process this new information they are gathering is necessary. We must listen to their concerns, their questions, and respond with sincere thoughts.

Forming Small Research Groups

When forming small groups, you can use the same protocols you typically use, if they work well. Typically for this exercise, I list the topics students will be researching on the board and allow students to self-select. This allows for them to feel ownership and have choice. It also ensures that they're doing what they want to do instead of simply completing a task I have assigned them. I begin by listing the topics and then assigning a number of group members next to it (Figure 3–5). As I call each topic out loud,

Chinese immigration	2 people
Chinese Exclusion Act	2 people
Chinatown and bubonic plague	3 people
Japanese internment camps	3 people
Chinese cultural beliefs and systems	4 people
Chinese American authors and Gene Luen Yang	2 people

Figure 3–5 Group and Topic Options

students raise their hands and I place their names next to the topics. When the target group number is reached, we move on. I always encourage students to have a second choice in the case that their first-choice topic is taken.

Research

This part of the process is important, too. In addition to learning about sources, summarizing, and synthesizing, this is a moment to teach about credibility. It is here where librarians can be of great support. They have systems and tools that can teach our students how to navigate digital research and pull out sources that are informative and accurate.

Additionally, it is during this research process where students might have necessary visceral reactions to the information they are consuming. Preparing yourself to deal with their emotions and reactions is important. Anyone "misbehaving" or showing troubling behaviors during this portion might in fact be expressing frustration due to the learning going on. This is also where community building can happen depending on how you, as the teacher, respond. I remember a conversation that started with a White female student and one of her group members as they were researching. We'll call them Tracy and Sarah. That conversation went something like this:

> **Tracy:** I can't believe I haven't known this all along. I can't believe that we White people have done all of this.
>
> **Me:** I know. It can be a hard history to accept. How do you feel?
>
> **Tracy:** I feel lied to and it makes me angry. I also feel confused.

Sarah: I feel confused, too. I feel guilty even though I haven't done anything.

Me: I can totally understand that. I get angry doing a lot of this research, myself. I get mad at the ways institutions have hurt all of us—whether by oppressing us or lying to those who oppress. In the end, oppressing others is hurtful to White people, too. It dehumanizes them since they are dehumanizing others. It's also allowing White people to walk around with lies that they think are truths.

Tracy: Yeah. That's true. I hadn't thought of it that way.

Sarah: What can I do? I'm not sure what to do.

Me: Let's check in with the larger group to see what others are thinking. I'm sure you're not alone in this.

At that point, I realized it was almost time to go and so I took some extra minutes and turned to all the students. I asked them how they were feeling as they were doing this research and of course many echoed Tracy and Sarah's sentiments. I used that moment to offer their frustration some hope by pointing out that they were already doing better by learning about this and that one way to beat this was by sharing their newfound knowledge. As they shared the truth with their peers, outside of our class, they were already working against the lies of White supremacy. This is the energy we need. We need to take their anger, their frustrations, their disappointment and encourage our students to turn that into fuel for action.

> We need to take their anger, their frustrations, their disappointment and encourage our students to turn that into fuel for action.

Present

Once their research is complete, and you've offered feedback and direction, helped them filter credible and quality sources, and removed unnecessary information, the groups present their findings/knowledge to the class. They end up teaching this content themselves, which is how we're decentered as teachers. This is another belief of Textured Teaching: students can be knowledge bearers and they can lead. Make sure to order and organize the presentations so that the information flows and is chronological. These presentations create the foundation needed to dive into the unit. They'll need to learn some things first to understand other things after. Without these lessons, students may be lost within a book or miss the deeper analytical power of a book as intended by the author.

Supplement and Think Critically

During a unit, a Textured Teacher finds ways to supplement the core text(s) with information that challenges students further than they thought the text(s) could go. These supplements may take the form of art work, mathematical data or statistics, science experiments, theatrical performances, and more. These are moments where the reading of the text is halted to dive deeply and look at aspects of the topic rarely explored through a unique lens. The goal of this exercise is to offer students a way to focus their study by integrating multiple sources that speak to one topic. This step in Textured Teaching enables students to see research come together and to make connections across various content areas.

Strategically find the moment where students have done enough research, have enough context, and have read enough of the text to pause. This might be halfway through a novel or even closer to the end. It's also usually tied to a moment in the text that highlights an injustice or a truth. Although this is assigned as a whole class, students can work in partners or small groups to (Read) Think, Pair, Share, while you confer with the partners or small groups to assess their comprehension and make sure big ideas are clear. Offering students guided questions for processing and analyzing is helpful. You can also use these answers as a formative assessment at this point in the unit.

When teaching Isabel Quintero's *Gabi, a Girl in Pieces* (2014), I supplement the text with various sources. Gabi, the main character, is a Mexican American young woman chronicling her last year of high school. Through writing and poetry, she forges her identity. Consider my current context: a predominantly White institution in Texas, a state with a large percentage of Mexicans/Mexican Americans, on a land that used to be Mexico and is still Indigenous, exploring and clarifying elements of her identity and experience are crucial. So, when we've reached a point where Gabi surfaces her racial identity issues and she crosses the border, we stop reading. This is an opportunity to go deep and learn beyond what the words on the page are telling us.

I introduce them to Gloria Anzaldúa, and we read an excerpt from her book *Border-lands/La Frontera* (2012). Anzaldúa does a phenomenal job of discussing the idea she calls "linguistic terrorism." It welcomes interesting dialogue for my students because it's often not something they've considered. It is a point of view that is very different from their own. Anzaldúa's text can easily fit into a history curriculum. It also ranges in genre, intentionally. In that way, it maintains the idea of interdisciplinary work because it's not perceived as a traditional English narrative. We then watch the music video "Soy Yo" by Bomba Estéreo (2017). This song channels the energy we watch Gabi develop throughout the book. The girl in the video gives us a visual representation of fictional Gabi. The song is in Spanish and that also adds to the richness of the interdis-ciplinary approach. We watch Residente's "Latinoamérica" (Calle 13 2010). This music video leads us to discuss the complexities of Latinx identity, which I use to lead us to discuss stereotyping and assumptions. The video incorporates art and that adds a layer of depth (and texture!) to the unit. Lastly, students watch and discuss the TEDx video "I'm Mexican. Does That Change Your Assumptions About Me?" (Vancour 2017). This "text" is an individual presentation that is nonfiction and yet another genre. Lastly, and this is after we returned to the book and finished reading, we watch the film *Real Women Have Curves* (Cardoso 2002) because we are able to watch a visual representa-tion of the motifs, characterization, and conflicts present in the book. The two texts (film and novel) seem to have been made for each other. They pair perfectly. Through these texts, I've centered the voices of the Latinx community, explored the injustices we face, questioned elements of racial ethnic identity, and offered students moments to consider their own. All of this happened through art, film, writing, and music. It surfaces great conversation that deals directly with the identity points Gabi articulates in the book. We watch these videos as a whole class and physically sit around the screen in a way that encourages discussion.

Is this something you feel confident taking on? If not, why not? What support do you need to get started? If you do, brainstorm the areas you feel confident engaging your students in.

This pause in the text and subsequent discussions with critical analysis offer students the opportunity to think about the real-life impact of the issues that the book surfaces. They are able to think about their own identities, issues of racial and ethnic identity, ways that systems have dictated people groups' identities, and how all of these historic systems are at work today. My White students, who make up the majority of my class, are able to gain an understanding of the challenges of race and racism for Latinxs in the United States. My students of color find space to share a bit of who they are, and if they don't want to share, they hear their story centered in the curriculum. A Textured Teaching structure to unit design ensures wholeness, engagement, and a focus on social justice. All of this happens in addition to traditional literary skill building such as identifying theme, analyzing motif, describing characterization, and more. Although this book doesn't focus on those particular skills, none of this work is in place of that work. It can all coexist, it's not mutually exclusive.

BOOK TITLE AND AUTHOR	SUMMARY	TERMS TO DEMYSTIFY AND DESTIGMATIZE
American Born Chinese, Gene Luen Yang (2006)	This multinarrative graphic novel, about a young Chinese American boy's search for cultural identity, is best used with eighth and ninth graders.	Race Racism Stereotypes Bias Prejudice Microaggressions
Gabi, a Girl in Pieces, Isabel Quintero (2014)	Written in diary form, this novel is about a young Mexican American girl's journey as a senior in high school as she grapples with her family, future, and identity. I think this text is best used in ninth to twelfth grades.	Ethnicity Culture Ethnic identity Latino/Latina Hispanic Latinx

Figure 3–6 Textured Teaching Units of Study: Interdisciplinary Samples

Figure 3-6 provides several examples of terms, research topics, and ways to supplement based on the text you're studying. The first column lists the book title, followed by the second column, which offers a brief summary of the text and states which grade level to try this with. The third column lists terms to discuss with students, and the fourth column lists research topics to take on before reading. The fifth column offers ideas for supplementing, and the last column helps you see the interdisciplinary areas that those supplements touch upon.

CONTEXTUAL RESEARCH TOPICS	SUPPLEMENTS	INTERDISCIPLINARY AREAS
Bubonic plague and Chinatown Chinese immigration Chinese Exclusion Act Chinatown Chinese authors, publications, and Gene Luen Yang Chinese cultural beliefs and systems Japanese internment camps	*Escape to Gold Mountain* (Wong 2012) *Becoming Americans* (Stavans 2009) *Fresh Off the Boat*, television series promotional video (Khan 2014) History of yellowface video (Vox 2016) Exclusion Act primary documents (Library of Congress 2020)	Visual arts Law History Poetry Sociology Anthropology Philosophy
Catholicism Matriarchal tendencies in Latin American cultures Machismo California Latinx graduation rates	"Linguistic Terrorism," (Anzaldúa 1995) "Latinoamérica," Residente (Calle 13 2010) "Soy Yo" (Bomba Estéreo 2017) *Real Women Have Curves* film (Cardoso 2002)	Sociology Anthropology Visual arts Music Psychology

continues

BOOK TITLE AND AUTHOR	SUMMARY	TERMS TO DEMYSTIFY AND DESTIGMATIZE
Return to Sender, Julia Alvarez (2009)	In this novel, two elementary-aged children grapple with the harsh realities of Mexican immigration and family hardships. I think this text is best used with sixth to eighth graders.	Immigration Smugglers Asylum Refugee Invasion Central America South America Caribbean Mexico Anti-immigrant sentiment Documentation Undocumented Illegal
In the Time of the Butterflies, Julia Alvarez (1995)	Based on a true story, this novel centers on three sisters fighting against Dominican dictator Rafael Trujillo. This text is best taught to tenth, eleventh, and twelfth graders.	Colorism Anti-Blackness Ethnic cleansing Patriarchy Power dynamic Governmental oppression

Figure 3–6 Textured Teaching Units of Study: Interdisciplinary Samples *(continued)*

CONTEXTUAL RESEARCH TOPICS	SUPPLEMENTS	INTERDISCIPLINARY AREAS
Mexican immigration history U.S. Immigration and Custom Enforcement (ICE) rules and regulations Deaths and illnesses at the border Smugglers and processes Indigenous migrants Vermont agriculture and immigration	"Thank You, Donald Trump!" (Ferrara 2016) *Karla Ortiz & Francesca Ortiz on Immigration* video (Democratic National Convention speech) (Ortiz and Ortiz 2016) *Dolores* film (Bratt 2018) "Migration Through Mexico" map (WOLA n.d.) Border, wall, and species report (Greenwald et al. 2017)	Law History Visual arts Geography Earth science
Leonidas Trujillo Trujillo regime Geography and history of the Dominican Republic Geography and history of Haiti Dominican migration and U.S. immigration patterns U.S. occupation of the Dominican Republic	Haitian massacre article (Bishop and Fernandez 2017) Invite a guest speaker to talk with your students TedEd video on Trujillo's rise and tensions with Haiti (Pichardo-Espaillat n.d.) *In the Time of the Butterflies* book (Alvarez 1995) and film (Barroso 2001)	Political science History Visual arts Geography

An Expansive View of Literacy

Blending the boundaries of content areas as young people learn serves many important needs including supporting emergent bilingual and multilingual students—students who are learning multiple languages, speak multiple languages already, and/or are working on developing their literacy skills in English—a growing demographic in the United States. When we have these students in our class, it can be a beautiful opportunity to learn with them and grow with them as a teacher, or it can be a painful period of implementing a harmful and neglectful curriculum on them. An interdisciplinary approach to literacy can work to counter mandated curriculum that is rigid and exclusive. Reading short stories offers opportunities for more voices in the curriculum, which grants these budding readers more access to diversity to identify what they like. Additionally, short stories offer the satisfaction of an achieved task, an important step in building reader confidence. Listening to sounds (music, noises featured in the text, etc.) that illuminate tone makes comprehension easier. Opportunities to work creatively offer more accessible ways for students to demonstrate their analysis. Watching clips of relevant videos enhances literacy connections. Moving at their pace, in a multisensory and interdisciplinary way, really helps students to comprehend and learn the new content that may have otherwise been inaccessible. For many young people, various stressors of their new lives create an overwhelming cognitive load that decreases processing capacity. They require a curriculum that slows down and allows for depth. Offering a range of paths to access information allows students to pick their own avenue to better internalize and own the classroom learning. Emergent bilingual and multilingual students in my classes have not only shown improvement in the (dreaded) state exams, but also developed tangible language gains both in English and in their home languages. Textured Teaching isn't just beneficial for "those" kids or the Black and Brown kids or the White kids or the underserved kids. It is for all students. Working toward justice in a pedagogically inclusive manner is for everyone.

> *Textured Teaching isn't just beneficial for "those" kids or the Black and Brown kids or the White kids or the underserved kids. It is for all students. Working toward justice in a pedagogically inclusive manner is for everyone.*

Collaborating with Colleagues

One of the most underrated tools we have at our fingertips is collaboration. It's really powerful for students to watch their teachers collaborate and admire each other's work, and it models an important skill they'll need in the professional world. For many reasons, collaboration is often an underused pedagogical tool, but I challenge us to find ways to make it work. I want teachers to consider how we can partner with colleagues who are experts, or at least well versed, in their content areas, and bring them into our class as guest speakers, contributors, or co-teachers of a unit. There are many ways to approach collaborating with colleagues. I offer three questions to consider before you reach out:

> *What ideas from another content area would be beneficial to under-stand or explore as we study this text?*
> Certain types of books lend themselves more easily to interdisciplinary work with particular content areas (shown in Figure 3–7). For example, when teaching a book that is highly descriptive, uses detailed imagery, focuses heavily on symbolism, or vividly creates settings for the reader, consider collaborating with a colleague in the arts department to create a visual representation of symbolic imagery from the text.
>
> *What insight does this colleague offer me in terms of what we will be studying?*
> Think of colleagues that are experts or at least have a breadth of knowledge on the subject matter. You don't even have to bring in the history teacher to talk about history-related topics. The art teacher might have great knowledge on the matter at hand and come in and speak on the historical content.
>
> *What prep should I do on my own to not create a burden or ask too much of my colleague?*
> This is important. Think of your own workload and what it might mean to have a colleague asking you to come and speak. Although you might really enjoy it, it does present additional work. Therefore, when inviting a colleague, do your best to think through what they will need and do some of your own research on the matter so you can offer them the opportunity to keep their talk brief and you can cover the rest, as much is possible.

TYPE OF BOOK	EXAMPLES	CONTENT AREA TO COLLABORATE WITH	COLLABORATION IDEAS
Books that are highly descriptive, using imagery and symbolism	*Krik? Krak!* (Danticat 1995) *Children of Blood and Bone* (Adeyemi 2018)	Art	Highlight artwork using symbols. Note artwork focusing on colors to analyze tone/mood. Discuss visual representation of analyses focusing on imagery or symbolism.
Books that focus on a historical time period, important social event, and/or require a sociopolitical background study	*Homegoing* (Gyasi 2016) *Fever 1793* (Anderson 2000)	History/social studies	Include essays that incorporate historical research. Ensure access to primary documents that would provide sociopolitical or historical context.
Science fiction books or books with scientific elements, events, or characters	*Kindred* (Butler 1979) *Frankenstein* (Shelley 1818)	Science	Host a class discussion featuring the guest (your colleague!) on the scientific elements featured in the book. Experiment day! *(In my Oprah Winfrey voice)* Welcome your colleague to the class where students experiment with the possibility of the scientific ideas present in the text.
Books that feature statistics, numerical data, or books that can be used to study a social issue where math is helpful	*Ghosts in the Schoolyard* (Ewing 2019) *Stamped: Racism, Antiracism, and You* (Reynolds and Kendi 2020)	Math	Invite your math colleague to help students sort out the numerical data offered in the book into visual charts for comprehension. Using the data, students have a discussion with your math colleague on the relationship between data, statistics, and bias. Through discussion, the math teacher can help students identify the most important or crucial data mentioned in the text.

Figure 3–7 Interdisciplinary Collaborations

You might be at a school where collaborating with coworkers isn't a thing and it's really not something that's a part of the culture. I'm sorry. Nothing stops you from heading over to social media and finding colleagues there. I've met and connected with educators across so many content areas on Twitter who I now consider part of my professional network. I've even had some of them join my class virtually as guest speakers. You can do this. We're all in this together.

Synthesizing and Debriefing with Students

As part of your Textured Teaching implementation, it's important to help students synthesize what they're learning and process the information. We want them to think about their thinking and understand that metacognitive work is a useful part of the process. Creating space to synthesize learning experiences shows how valuable debriefing can be while also building community among students and between them and the teacher. Sharing ideas might help students process their own and allow them to build on others' ideas, but I know you know this.

Synthesizing a whole learning experience can be challenging, but also satisfying. One effective way of synthesizing is to have students create visual representations of their learning through mind maps. They can categorize information, make word webs of the ideas they are internalizing, or create lists stating their understandings. Either way, helping them to sort out their thinking and drawing connections throughout the unit is a helpful way to synthesize. I have found the following prompts helpful when I'm synthesizing with students especially after these interdisciplinary learning journeys.

- "What relationships can you identify across the different texts we used to learn about this topic?" (This requires an expansive understanding of text.)
- "How are all of the topics we've explored connected in some way?"
- "Go back in your notes and highlight all the keywords you think are the most important from this unit. Then, take the words and put them in some type of order."
- "Dump all the words and concepts we've learned during this unit on the board. Together, as a class, add, modify, remove, and improve that list."

After synthesizing, you can require students to submit something in writing with their final evaluation and debrief. Some ways to do this are through a whole-class debrief of the unit, a unit evaluation via a Google Form, and others. You can solicit students' feedback for improvement in your instruction and unit design. I often offer various prompts (Figure 3–8) and students can choose which one to respond to. This allows for choice, but also ensures that you ask what you want.

- What could I have done better in this unit to help you learn more information and ideas?
- What overall grade would you give this unit and why?
- What changes should I make to this unit when considering teaching it again next year?
- What was most effective in this unit for you? What was least effective?

Figure 3–8 Prompts for Reflection

Teaching young people through interdisciplinary ways can model for students how institutions make systems, too. What I mean is that if I can understand how science and arts come together and elucidate concepts in a sci-fi book, I can also open my mind to see how problems in health care and the economy might come together to lead to larger social issues, too. It helps students make connections. In following this line of thinking, another way to help students really integrate ideas and internalize learning is to make it physical. Help them feel it, see it, hear it, smell it, taste it, and therefore remember it. A Textured Teacher also makes learning experiential.

Do you incorporate this practice in your pedagogy now? How is student voice and choice present in your curricular design?

CAUTIONS AND CHALLENGES

Challenge:
You struggle with quality and lengthy access to the internet or computer use.

The struggle is real, especially in underfunded schools. Some suggestions include: print articles, make copies of excerpts/pages, go to the library as a class, bring in books, welcome guest speakers, visit a local museum, contact a local college professor willing to help with building background via a class interview, and so on. Getting creative with this is key.

Challenge:
You don't have time to spare due to standardized testing or lack of autonomy in general.

Find ways to do things simultaneously or jigsaw this work. For example, have a couple of students do demystifying and destigmatizing, have another small group do background building, and have the last group do more technical/literary prep work. This might cut up the process into days versus weeks. You'll also have to determine what you can do. It's OK to accept that we can't do it all.

Adding a Layer of Texture

Teachers who are bilingual or multilingual have a great advantage. We don't always know how to incorporate that aspect of our identity into our instruction. I want us to consider bringing in texts in our home/native/spoken languages other than English that connect in some way to the core text or unit of study. We might need to translate that work/text or find its English version. It would be so dope to include them and have conversations about texts in translation, interpretation and translation, word choice, and more. I have found that when I do that it creates trust between students and me because not only do they learn more about me, but they also learn more about my skills and knowledge. We model for them how to be confident in who they are and that who we are counts in the classroom. When I use Spanish, it certainly adds depth and richness, but it demonstrates my language and literacy skills. It shows a lot of the work I can do, and when I flex that muscle, I teach students that bilingualism and biliteracy are gems, power, and beautiful. This might easily be contrary to what their own bilingualism is being portrayed as to them. They trust me more because they learn about what I know and what I can teach them. Through this strategy you're not only adding more texture to the unit, but you're adding more of yourself.

Notes

TEXTURED TEACHING IS EXPERIENTIAL

> "Teachers are not performers in the traditional sense of the word in that our work is not meant to be a spectacle. Yet it is meant to serve as a catalyst that calls everyone to become more and more engaged, to become active participants in learning.
>
> —bell hooks, *Teaching to Transgress*

Learning should be engaging and involve all of ourselves as much as possible. As Dr. Tim San Pedro explains, "When curriculum affirms the identities of students through the development of critical intellectualism, students increase their motivation and engagement in schooling contexts" (Paris and Alim 2017, 101). Critical intellectualism, which refers to rigorous analytical thinking that goes beyond surface level ideas, involves thinking critically and analytically about the world around you. Essentially, experiential learning.

Dr. Hammond writes about pushing students to and through a productive struggle into cognitive growth (Hammond 2014), including relationship building and other social and emotional skills. To summarize a neurocognitive process, when presented with new information, the brain decides and deciphers what information to retain, codes the new information in a way that makes it memorable and meaningful, and then transfers the knowledge and applies the new learning. Experiential learning brings a student through all of these steps by expanding the limits of the classroom and incorporating sensorial experiences, making the learning physical and memorable.

The Community as a Resource

To welcome the city or community as a classroom, you have to see the community through an asset-based perspective as a place that is full of valuable resources. This may be easier to do in some communities but for many students, specifically students of color, the dominant narrative about their communities often focuses on ways in which the community is lacking. Take my hometown, for example. Lawrence, Massachusetts is a small, seven-square-mile city full of Dominicans, Puerto Ricans, and other Black, Brown, and Asian immigrants. Although many of the residents were business owners or held professional degrees in their home countries, their degrees were not recognized in the United States and their professional experiences were not welcomed or seen, limiting their job opportunities within their fields here. The local newspaper regularly presented Lawrence only through narratives of struggle, loss, defeat, and failure. That deficit-based narrative shaped the perspective of people from outside the community, including the teachers who came in to teach my peers and me. This may be my personal experience, but it is also one that I know is shared by many who come from similar settings and contexts as I did. An asset-based perspective counters the negative narrative and brings a positive self-view and sense of affirmation for students. Paolo Freire describes the process of building consciousness to transform an oppressive system:

> The truth is, however, that the oppressed are not "marginals," are not people living "outside" society. They have always been "inside"— inside the structure which made them "beings for others." The solution is not to "integrate" them into the structure of oppression, but to transform that structure so that they can become "beings for themselves." (2000, 74)

A teacher who understands the richness and knowledge of a community can have a hugely positive impact on a student. It helps students shift their gaze and start to experience their community as a place where learning can happen. When we make connections from the classroom to the outside world, we are teaching young people to be aware, socially conscious, and lifelong learners.

Creating Learning Experiences for Students

You can create learning experiences for students that help them reimagine themselves, understand others, and think critically about how to transform the systems in place in our country. Literature provides us with a unique opportunity to help students visit places they've never visited, meet people they may never have had contact with, and listen to stories that are different from their own. For students of color, it is important to experience stories that open their eyes and mind outside of the often narrow narratives presented about themselves. Black students need to see stories where they are not enslaved, where instead there is joy, peace, action, and power. Latinx students need to experience stories where they see themselves as complex characters not reduced to stereotypical immigrants, pregnant teen girls, sexy women, or overworked, silent men. Indigenous students need stories where they are the authors, where they tell of their resilience, strength, and beauty—where they exist in a triumphant present and not a mythic past. Asian American students need stories that show the totality of their identities, including those of Southeast Asians, both immigrants and families here for generations, and love stories. How many Asian American young adult love stories can you name? White students need to see all of those stories, too. They also need to see themselves as racialized people, descendants of colonizers, with the opportunity to dismantle what their ancestors created. We must empower them with the hope of revolution. By turning our classrooms into experiential learning opportunities, we create moments for students to see a new side of themselves and others and envision a truer society.

You can begin to incorporate this experiential approach by tapping into local agencies, nonprofits, or organizations that can bring to life aspects to be studied during your unit. Many local museums have educational guides or people who lead educational activities. I know you probably know this, but I'm just here to show love to these museums. I typically check museums, libraries, art galleries, and community center calendars. I look for activities or events that can connect in any way to what we are learning about in class. The most critical part of those outings is the ride back to school. I often invite students into reflection, sometimes written (on their phones) or discussed with their bus buddies. I offer reflection and debriefing prompts to engage them to make academic connections. When our class meets again, those prompts are the starting point. It's a good way to pick up where we left off and start with their voices.

You can also welcome the voices of community members that connect to your content. Often, English classrooms feel restrictive and stiff because they overwhelmingly involve reading and writing while sitting quietly at desks. This is a good opportunity to move out of the desks, get into a community circle, and listen. We drop our pens and open our ears. These guests are authentic voices that can enhance our comprehension of the content we're exploring. When reaching out to guests, I share what we're learning about, but more importantly, I try to offer them a specific topic I want them to address with students. This is especially helpful for people who are not public speakers or don't typically interact with students. For them, these visits can be uncomfortable, so whatever we can do to support them during their visit helps.

Shifting that experience by taking students outdoors or by being present in the local community begins to show them how learning doesn't have to be only one way. Learning doesn't only exist within the four walls of the classroom, in those seats, in that school. Learning can happen at the park; it can happen on a city bus; it can take place at the local library. One of the most important aspects of heading outside is the preparation and planning that teachers must do. You need to think through the steps of the trip. Some questions that guide me in this planning include:

- What items will the students need in terms of academics and weather? I make sure to communicate this to students and parents beforehand.
- What items will I need?
- What supports would be helpful and what do I need to set that up?
- What do I need to keep in mind for safety reasons? Could I use a chaperone? If so, who? If not, what issues could arise that I need to prepare for?

Thinking through the steps of an outing I used to take regularly with a class became a safety issue. During this outing is when I used to take a class of mine to the local library. It was a five-minute walk up a hill next to our building. Although the walk was easy and the trip was short, around the side of the library where we used to walk, there were also people experiencing homelessness that would spend their time in that area. There were some men in particular who would sexually harass some of the girls in my class, myself included. After encountering this for the first time, I knew that we needed to change our route to avoid them. This preplanning makes all the difference when it comes to a successful outing.

A Sensorial Approach

The five senses are a great way to approach this experiential learning. Teaching a text by incorporating ways for students to see it, touch it, taste it, hear it, and smell it can be invigorating as well as inspiring. Consider spending a day outdoors while reading, especially if the text you're exploring has moments outdoors. For example, when reading *The Adventures of Huckleberry Finn* (Twain 1998), I walked with students to the Colorado River where we did some reading, writing, and group work to imagine what Huck and Jim might have experienced moving along the vastness of the Mississippi River. I also wanted students to consider the dangers Jim was exposed to as a runaway formerly enslaved person and how the imminence of that danger was present on the shore. Students standing beside the Colorado River were able to see a large body of water, like the one in the text. They were able to smell what the area might have been like for Huck and Jim. Students touched the ground, felt the cold water, walked past the branches, and physically felt what the space was like. They could hear the birds, the water, the people, the leaves, the wind, and try to immerse themselves in dreaming about life on the water. Although they couldn't taste anything, they could imagine the types of food they must have eaten based on what was available. Not only is this highly engaging and participatory, but it also makes the text memorable and allows for critical and close reading in deep ways. If you know your students, you can design experiential lessons that appeal to their specific interests, allowing you to invite all students to engage with the material.

Sight

We want students to be able to visualize scenes and moments from the text to ensure full comprehension and lead them to critical analysis. To help students see a text, you can use film adaptations, short videos, documentaries, or other visual arts that amplify moments, setting, themes, and motifs from the texts. For students, seeing the same idea across different forms and genres can be quite helpful to open different pathways toward deep, critical analysis. For example, when reading *Night* by Elie Weisel (1960), we also studied artist Joseph Cornell's work, The Joseph Cornell Box. These are a type of shadow boxes that focus on quotidian objects and place them in an artistic assemblage. Students selected a short passage from Weisel's memoir, no longer than a paragraph, to focus on. They paid attention to all of the descriptive language, sensory details, verbs, and overall mood of the passage. They then created a box that reflected that analysis through the use of carefully selected objects, colors, and textures. Through this assignment, students practiced close reading and analytical skills. Figure 4–1 shows a box created by a ninth-grade student as part of this *Night* unit.

Additionally, Deborah Roberts, a talented and critical Black woman artist, uses mixed media to represent social commentary and offer a critique of our commonly held notions of beauty. She challenges stereotypes and myths and uses her art to

Figure 4–1 *Night* Box

create dialogue centered on women. You can use her work with many texts, including *Night*, to help your students see how art can bring all of this together in creative and tactile ways. This is why "what" students see is also crucial to Textured Teaching, not just "how."

Similarly, the *Codex Espangliensis* (2000) offers a powerful opportunity to shift students' thinking on what counts as a text, what a text can be, and how it can be read. Created by Guillermo Gómez-Peña, Enrique Chagoya, and Felicia Rice, the *Codex Espangliensis* is an accordion-shaped text inspired by early Indigenous codices, which had escaped destruction by colonizers. In this modern text, there are all forms of genre writing, artistic montages, voices, and imagery that come together to tell the history of a people, nationalism, and violent interactions. It is over twenty feet long and can be read in any direction because there isn't a beginning or end. Cool, right? The book's physical structure can spark great dialogue with your students about what we see and know as normal in our society when it comes to the written word and literature, in general. When I read it with students, I usually take the class outside and display the book on the floor, which, contrary to how we are used to reading, requires they get uncomfortable and adjust themselves to the book. The reader is centered in the typical reading experience. The codex, though, shifts that power dynamic because it cannot be held or used like a traditional book. Not only is this a very physical experience, but the visual creativity and diversity that the text brings together is a challenge for students. It requires us to imagine what the authors are trying to communicate. It also calls each reader in differently because each page can be read in so many ways. Our eyes are drawn to various elements, and there are so many options to where you want to start and how you want to make sense of that page in relation to the others. By pushing students in these ways, we push them to imagine and invent new ways of reading, sharing, and seeing the world.

There are many ways to do this work of including learning that is multisensory, but that depends on how much autonomy you have as a teacher in your school and district. If you have minimal autonomy, then through supplementing (see Chapter 3), you can bring in voices marginalized and neglected by English classrooms. If you have full autonomy, then I would invite you to search online and discuss your opportunities with fellow educators to diversify your curriculum and text selections. If you find yourself in the middle ground where you have some autonomy, but not full ability, to design your entire curriculum, then be empowered to make bold choices for the sake of your students and our future. Know that what the institutions require will often mainly feature White, cis-gendered, and straight voices. Be unapologetically intentional about selecting books that offer different and beautiful perspectives that will expand your students' racialized imaginations. This can be done. So many of us are doing this consistently and openly. You can do it, too.

Sound

In the continued fight for justice, who and what we hear in the classroom should welcome ideas and voices that have historically been marginalized and rejected. This means welcoming guest speakers who may not be traditionally considered academic and embracing their contributions as meaningful. Speakers can be members of students' families or community members. It requires that you work diligently to create equity of narratives by ensuring voices historically ignored, and in some cases vilified, through schooling are heard.

Welcoming visitors is a profoundly enhancing element to Textured Teaching that brings a richness to class discussions and deepens community building. In particular, consider guests that have non-American accents, for whom English isn't their first language, or who speak an English other than the dominant one. These voices create a sense of auditory texture through their complexities and encourage students to shift their understanding about who and what gets to be discussed in school. While being careful to not tokenize a person, you start to show whose voices you value and consider important when you do this. Students start to understand that anyone can be engaged on these topics and that we all, in fact, have thoughts and opinions worthy of discussing. For example, I have included many guests to join our classes consistently for many years for all of the reasons you'll hear me outline in this chapter. When reading *In the Time of the Butterflies* by Julia Alvarez (1995) with predominantly Latinx students, I invite my father to join our classes and tell stories of the dictator discussed in the story, share some of the historical and political context of the time, and make international connections for us between the Dominican Republic and other countries. One year, while reading *American Born Chinese* by Gene Luen Yang (2006), I had the father of one of my Chinese

How does welcoming guest voices to your classroom sound? Overwhelming, exciting, interesting, impossible, or manageable?

international students join us (he was coincidentally on a trip) and share about the Monkey King. One year, as I taught *Night* (Weisel 1960), one of my students' fathers was working on writing the book that shares the story of his own grandfather as a soldier in World War II. Lastly, on one occasion I had a former graduate professor talk about Black English, its structure, and its value. Figure 4–2 shares guiding questions to help you determine how to invite a guest or welcome a voice.

Sound also includes music. Many teachers enjoy using classical or instrumental music in the background as students work. That can be conducive to a productive learning environment. I encourage you to expand your idea of music as more than simply background noise and consider it a full element of the classroom learning. Through Textured Teaching, you can use any type of music to explore lyrics and also create connections to a text for students: pop music or international music, older or newer, well known or underground. The use of hip-hop, in particular, can be a revolutionary act. Because of its origins in the Black community (in partnership with the Latinx community), anti-Black sentiment keeps it in a sphere where many consider it to be unacademic. Another hesitation for using hip-hop is due to its language and often sexual or misogynistic content. This is a real issue, but here is where I stand on that:

- What moment in the text do I want to bring to life through a guest?
- What people group does this book center, and who can I welcome to speak to the complexities of this identity?
- Who are these main characters, and what minor characters are we not hearing from? Who in this community might shed light on that minor character's point of view?
- What voices are missing in this text? *Find a community member to fill in that void.*
- What incident in the text needs more contextualizing, and who in this community might have direct experience? What local organizations can be a resource for this?

Figure 4–2 Inviting a Guest

students (in general) are already listening to it. Why not delete the foul language (as you print lyrics) and help them use their critical and academic lens to discuss popular culture? As a genre, hip-hop is a rich and genius opportunity to promote literacy and critical analysis. It's also a powerful tool for discussing culture and learning how to use the word to read the world.

Not only does hip-hop offer lessons in the grammatical structure and patterns of African American Vernacular English (Smitherman 1995), but it provides a lens into Black America and leads us to question White American values and culture. It's both a linguistic and cultural classroom in its own right. Hip-hop is also a genre of hopes and dreams. These are hopes for a better tomorrow and dreams for a whole community. Writing prompts inspired by hip-hop are also a good way to welcome marginalized voices as well as open the door for freewriting in the classroom. Freewriting often builds rapport between students and teachers. It is important not to consider hip-hop as a bridge to "complex texts" or as a tool to get students engaged to dig into what it is you really want to do. That becomes a gimmick, and hip-hop ain't a gimmick. I strongly encourage against this. When you do this, you are communicating to students that such music and content are only good for the reaching of other content, as a lens to look at other things, rather than as content that is valuable in and of itself. It can feel like a trick to catch students and get them to do what you really want, which can easily break rapport and disrupt the trust you've been working on building.

There are many ways to incorporate hip-hop in English language arts classrooms. You can offer students hip-hop as texts weaved into units, analyzing lyrics to draw direct connections to a text you're studying. It can be used as a supplement. You can have a poetry and hip-hop unit where you explore both poetry and hip-hop and use a poetic analysis approach to both texts. You can also offer a hip-hop-only unit or a hip-hop-only course. Dr. Marc Lamont Hill offers us a course outline of Hip Hop Lit in *Beats, Rhymes, and Classroom Life* (2009). He explains that his purpose in the course and his work included analyzing "the ways in which youth use hip hop texts as complex sites of identity work" (xvii). Hip-hop, as mentioned previously, can be used to understand our students, to help them understand life, and to help them see our social issues clearer. Hill makes the argument that hip-hop can be used to analyze our society and also center student voices. "I wanted Hip Hop Lit to allow the experiences of the students and the authors to be the centerpiece of the course" (18).

Using hip-hop is an approach that counts for all students. Considering how hip-hop is now the dominant genre since 2017 (McIntyre 2017), most of your students are listening to this music. Hill goes on to explain that "in the humanities, hip hop scholars have relied upon close readings of hip hop texts, particularly rap music and videos, to show how they reflect and inform particular forms of gender . . . race . . . and political economy" (4). Figure 4–3 offers ways to incorporate music, including hip-hop, as supplements to texts studied in the classroom.

What are some of your biases toward or against hip-hop? Write about your exposure and/or experience with hip-hop and what you need to do to incorporate it into your curriculum.

MAIN TEXT	SONGS	ANALYSIS
The Poet X, Elizabeth Acevedo (2018) *A novel in verse about a young woman exploring her identity and the power of poetry* (grades 9–12)	"Bachata Rosa" by Juan Luis Guerra (bachata) "Carta de Amor" by Juan Luis Guerra (bachata) "Girl on Fire" by Alicia Keys (pop music)	Consider the poetic elements present in these songs that mirror the ones present in *The Poet X*. The first two songs can be used to think about relationships, since they are such an important part of who Xiomara is becoming. The last song could be used to study her characterization and could be seen as an expression of herself.
The Hate U Give, Angie Thomas (2017) *A novel centering a young Black woman's struggle between two worlds in the midst of police brutality* (grades 9–12)	"Changes" by Tupac Shakur (hip-hop) "Brenda's Got a Baby" by Tupac Shakur (hip-hop) "Keep Ya Head Up" by Tupac Shakur (hip-hop)	Since Tupac Shakur is present in the text, you can explore his music. The lyrics of these three songs lend themselves to a discussion of the issues and concerns present in the Black community and ones that come up for Starr and her family, friends, and community. Think about both content and form, analyzing not only for literary techniques, but also thinking critically about the theme. "Changes" could be a springboard into a study of American economics.

Figure 4–3 Ideas for Incorporating Sound *(continues)*

MAIN TEXT	SONGS	ANALYSIS
The House on Mango Street, Sandra Cisneros (1991) *A novel in vignettes about a young Mexican American girl exploring her identity, learning about her community, and dreaming through writing.* (grades 6-9)	"I Can" by Nas (hip-hop) "Everything Is Everything" by Lauryn Hill (hip-hop)	Both of these songs are about youth experiences in challenging neighborhoods. Nas includes an uplifting message and attempts to inspire young people, and Lauryn Hill paints a picture of what it means to endure while considering one's history. Both songs offer opportunities for close reading exercises where a thematic analysis can be connected to the main text.
Long Way Down, Jason Reynolds (2017) *A novel in prose about family, gun violence, and the complexity of that cycle* (grades 8–10)	"Self-Destruction" by Stop the Violence Movement (hip-hop) "No Guns Allowed" by Snoop Lion (hip-hop) "I Gave You Power" by Nas (hip-hop)	Gun violence is an issue that continues to face U.S. society today, and it's an especially relevant topic in schools. All three songs offer opportunities for analysis of the intersection of race and gun violence. The last song in particular, by Nas, can be used as a mentor text. It's told from the point of view of the gun.
Persepolis: The Story of a Childhood, Marjane Satrapi (2004) *A graphic novel following the life of the author during the Iranian Revolution in the 1980s* (grades 9–12)	"Fight the Power" by Public Enemy (hip-hop) "Bin Laden" by Immortal Technique (hip-hop)	Resisting government oppression and problematic policies are at the foundation of U.S. society. Both of these songs offer opportunities for analysis and a window into resistance. The first song can be a mentor text, and you can grant students opportunities to write their own song. The second song can be used for conversation about how artists use their platforms to share awareness and their political ideas.

Figure 4–3 Ideas for Incorporating Sound *(continued)*

Smell, Taste, and Feel

Although sight and sound are easy elements to integrate, smell, taste, and feel are a bit more challenging. How can you get students to smell, taste, and feel ideas, words, and experiences harbored in a flat book? It requires intentional preparation and planning.

Smelling and tasting what characters in the book smell and taste, or what authors describe for readers, is challenging when it's not an explicit detail in the narrative. For example, if the story includes food, then it's easy to re-create the smell and taste for students by having the food in class. This is especially helpful if the story's food is symbolic or important to the plot. If the story includes a visit to a specific place, like a zoo or a beach, then you can make direct connections to those smells and draw on students' prior experiences, if they have them. However, books don't always feature moments that bring attention to smell or taste. In such a scenario, then, you might not focus on smell or taste.

Feeling, however, is a fun opportunity to practice creativity. Some of my favorite teaching moments are when students are able to feel what characters feel and sense what a setting might feel like. When thinking about how to get students to feel a moment in the story, I always want to make sure that the exercise physically takes them out of their seats—maybe even out of the comforts of the physical classroom. These moments involve activities such as taking a ride on the city bus, sitting on the floor while getting (lightly) sprayed with a water bottle, standing out in the hot Texas sun during a walk, finding fake body parts across campus, and more. Usually, these experiences result in laughter, and they certainly set the students up for wanting to know and understand the characters even more.

Bringing the Text to Life

Your thoughtful ideas and creative ways to enhance the text and bring it to life will be necessary for this element of Textured Teaching. You have options on how to do this, keeping in mind that this is about getting our students to think about how to positively transform our society. You've selected texts that are inclusive of voices excluded by the traditional canon, and you've helped students to see the text and hear it in new ways. You also, now, will help students experience the text in a way that will allow them to see the relevance of this to them, their society, and their future. Often students ask us questions such as "Why are we doing this?" or "Why does this matter?" and a Textured Teaching approach answers by showing.

Bringing the text to life allows students the chance to see, hear, smell, taste, and feel elements of a moment or scene. To do this, it requires identifying a moment or scene that is either crucial for comprehension or foreign to your students. Although visiting a local space can be awesome, it can also be challenging because it requires you to coordinate things like transportation, permission slips, potential costs, and chaperones. A key trick I use for permission slips is that I have one permission slip at the start of the year that covers the whole year. Parents then know that our class will often be off-site. I do communicate when we're leaving and where we're headed, but unless they contact me, their student has permission to attend the trip. Of course, it's necessary for you to discuss all of this at the start of the year with your school leader. Figure 4–4 is a sample permission slip I've used in the past for a semester course I taught.

At our school, we have a digital platform where teachers and parents can communicate. We also use an email system. What I do is communicate several days, even

PERMISSION SLIP

I give permission for my child _____ to be off campus with Lorena Germán, throughout the semester. I am aware that field trips will be listed on XXXXXX and that I can contact her via email or XXXXXXX if I have any questions. I am also aware that she will sign the class out at the front desk to ensure safety with school officials and administrators.

I am also fully aware that the course content will be challenging and may surface controversial and challenging topics and that my child may have questions and/or concerns about them. I am aware that I can reach out to Lorena about questions regarding content and can seek clarification from her as well.

Date _____

Parent/guardian name _____

Parent/guardian signature_____

Figure 4–4 Sample Permission Slip

a week in advance, about when we are heading out so parents are aware. I let them know why we're going, how it connects to the content, and if necessary, I ask for chaperones. If your school does not have these communication means, then try gathering emails or phone numbers at the start of the year so you can send a mass message to parents informing them of what's coming up. Keeping parents in the loop of what's going on in your class is only beneficial because it keeps those lines of communication open and you never know what resources they can offer for learning as well.

Identifying Moments in the Text

Now, in the case that leaving is not what you'll do, what scenes should you focus on to create an experiential learning moment for your students? That's always a tough question, but I have arrived at some answers. It's important to focus on moments that help students comprehend and analyze characterization, theme, setting, plot, or social justice or make text-to-self connections. I focus on those six concepts because not only do they support a reader's comprehension (Serravallo 2018), but they enable us to analyze a text and see it in context of the reader's world. Moments to look for include ones that:

- reveal an important trait about characters (characterization)
- reveal important details about place and time (setting)
- mark a turning point in the story (plot)
- speak to issues of inclusivity, race, or social justice (theme and social justice)
- present experiences that are unfamiliar to your students (connections).

Another way to think about how to enhance students' comprehension to push them to engage deeply is by considering seven areas of comprehension (Serravallo 2018):

1. Determining importance
2. Inferring/interpreting
3. Synthesizing/retelling
4. Questioning
5. Visualizing
6. Activating prior knowledge
7. Utilizing fix-up strategies.

In her book, *Understanding Texts & Readers,* Jennifer Serravallo (2018) digs deep into what each of these areas is and how to help students understand texts better. I offer them as a way to guide your design for experiential learning as part of your Textured Teaching. Experiencing these moments not only will make the text relevant, but will expose your students to moments that may have otherwise gone unnoticed. Figure 4–5 offers some questions to ask yourself as you try to implement this part of Textured Teaching.

- What moment reveals a depth of this character my students need to notice?
- What in this narrative might be foreign to my students, and how I can help them empathize?
- What in this narrative might be foreign to my students and be a source of disconnect for them?
- What was a turning point in the plot that I need to help students see? How can I slow us down so we can notice that?
- What element of the setting is crucial for students to understand so they can better understand the plot/conflict/character?
- What is a theme in this text I want students to notice and what feeling is it connected to? What experience might offer this feeling?
- What moment in this story speaks to a larger social (in)justice issue that I can focus on for my students?

Figure 4–5 Questions for Selecting a Moment in a Text

Sensitivity and Intentionality

When creating these experiences for your students, particularly from texts featuring painful stories, it's important to consider how not to glorify these situations and to maintain a sense of curiosity and sobriety. These may be real people in real situations enduring trauma and pain. If it's based on a fictional character, it's still stemming from lived experiences. If the whole story is fictional and what you're re-creating is fully fictional, then all you need to be concerned about is not engaging in an activity that may trigger students who have experienced something painful related to this activity. For example, if you're reading science fiction and you'll be re-creating a moment where you take off on a magic ship headed to a magical land, you might have students who have a fear of planes or flight. Be careful and thoughtful, and overcommunicate.

But if you're reading a book that falls into the realistic fiction genre, then keep in mind that these are real circumstances that people are struggling through. It's important for you to explicitly communicate that to your students and encourage them to treat the experience/exercise with that tenderness and gravity. If not, it ends up being a "fun" experience that was funny or silly, and opens up the space for potentially insensitive and offensive comments.

As amazing as these activities can be, there's also a thin line between learning and hurting. There is a difference between a simulation and creating a text-based physical learning experience. What I do with students might include a replica of some elements of the text. Sometimes, I try to physically create a moment, event, or object for the purpose of seeing, understanding, or analyzing. A simulation, on the other hand, requires a sense of deception because you are attempting to pretend and imitate a situation or event. That pretend play is where the risk of harm and offense creeps in. Therefore, it's important to know what not to do, not to re-create, and certainly not simulate in your Textured Teaching classroom. Although there is a lot of freedom with what you can do, there are important boundaries you should set for yourself. There are many scenarios that are wrong to simulate or re-create in your classroom. Avoid scenarios that

- re-create oppressive structures
- single out individual students or whole student groups based on their identity
- present identities as topics of debate
- expose marginalized students to further harm
- ask students to act like a particular group of people, especially marginalized ones
- create opportunities for students to stereotype or dehumanize others.

> *This is often a reality teachers try to avoid. How do you feel about engaging in this work and potentially facing this scenario? What work do you need to do beforehand to prepare for exercises like these?*

I would advise you to stay away from historical reenactments that include elements of the list on page 87. Those elements are often found, for example, in scenarios that involve enslaved people-related simulations. Slavery is not something to ever simulate in your classroom for many reasons. We are in a country that has not come to terms with slavery, offered reparations, or promoted healing. Bringing that period to life is harmful, painful, and never something to play with or try to turn into a classroom activity. It is a great topic for study, discussion, and reflection, but not for "experiencing." Hasan Kwame Jeffries, history professor and host of Teaching Hard History by Learning for Justice, explains that we should not create simulations of events related to "the holocaust, slavery, war crimes, or any other event where people experienced violence or trauma" (Gonzalez 2019). In the same vein, any scenario that asks students to engage in blackface, perform stereotypes, act like "immigrants," act like any group, especially marginalized ones, is usually a dangerous opportunity for students to hurt others and practice stereotypes. These are not moments where they get to imagine a new United States of America or rectify wrongdoings of our past. Figure 4-6 presents questions to ask yourself as you consider whether or not to do an experiential activity.

- Might any student in the classroom be offended by this?
- Might any parent be offended by this?
- Does this activity require the singling out of one or more students in the group based on an element of their identity that they cannot control?
- Does this activity maintain a historically oppressive structure present in our society?
- Does this activity uphold White supremacy by furthering the current power dynamic of White students as powerful and students of color as powerless?
- Does this activity exclude or potentially cause shame for a student's gender, sexual, or other identity?

Figure 4–6 Questions for Determining Next Steps

If the questions give you pause and if you're at all unsure, consider discussing this project idea with a colleague or mentor. Consider researching this idea online to see what other educators have said about it. It is so important that in our quest for providing rich learning experiences we don't re-create the harmful experiences our marginalized students are enduring outside of our classroom/school walls. This continues to require work from us, preparation, research, and thoughtfulness. Our students deserve that. Our futures need it.

A key component to Textured Teaching is debriefing. You want to have a conversation where you process with students what they experienced, what they learned, how that moment helped them understand what the character may have been going through and what real people may be experiencing in the world. Our students don't always know all of the problems that exist or how they feel about them. How can we expect them to change these problems? Use Figure 4–7 to outline some questions you can use to debrief with students.

An Example from My Class

One unit where I found a critical disconnect for my students happened while reading *Incidents in the Life of a Slave Girl* by Harriet Jacobs (1861). In this narrative by a Black woman, formerly enslaved, we learn about her journey through slavery and eventual escape. Her story is amazing, powerful, and full of examples of resilience and beauty. Part of her story is that she first escapes from slavery by actually staying in the very town where she had been enslaved. She hid in an attic space of her grandmother's house for approximately seven years. We did not simulate any of the aspects of her story, but what we did do to better understand setting and characterization was re-create the attic space where she hid for her life. Although my class was quite diverse that year, featuring international students, none of them had experienced hardships like hers or had to live in any condition that resembled this in any way. The disconnect between my students and Harriet was glaring.

As I mentioned, to better understand her story, the period, the conflicts, her character, and the setting, we set out to re-create the attic in which she had hid. Students got into several groups. One group set out to build the attic space. Another group worked on identifying lines and quotes from the text, along with research, to use

- What were you feeling during this experience?
- What did this experience reveal to you about the character/moment that you had not considered before?
- What did this experience reveal to you about what you don't know?
- What is a subject that you'd like to learn more about as a result of this exercise?
- Is there any experience that you have endured that you think might have some, even if minor, parallels to this experience?
- What type of support do you think this character/people in these cir-cumstances might need?

Figure 4–7 Questions for Debriefing with Students

on the attic. The builders group took Jacobs' descriptions and built a structure that closely resembled her hiding space. We used boxes and cardboard we found around campus to create the structure. I purchased some sticks at the hardware store to hold our structure up. We used paint that one of the students found at home, and after about two weeks we had built the space. The researchers had created a collection of quotes about her time in the attic, research to support our analysis of the Fugitive Slave Act, and other texts that gave voice to the struggles and stories of enslaved women. The content was both on the outside and the inside of the structure. Although students did venture into the structure, the focus of the exercise was not to try and "experience what she had experienced." That would be impossible and open the door to problematic activities in the classroom.

Have you ever considered a sensorial approach to teaching English? If so, how? If not, what do you think might be both your strengths and challenges in implementing this? Who can be a partner in this work for you?

When I debriefed with students the exercise from *Incidents in the Life of a Slave Girl*, I used some of the questions in Figure 4-7. Specifically, I asked the first and second ones. I wanted students to potentially empathize with Jacobs by considering the struggle of her hiding spot to highlight how bad her experience as an enslaved person must have been to endure those seven years in that small space. First, I had students partner off and share their responses through brief discussion. Once I saw that all students had shared and that discussion was blossoming, I gathered everyone and turned it into a whole-class discussion. I simply restated the same questions to the whole group. Once everyone shared, I also engaged them in a conversation about refugees in general and pushed them to try and make connections with other scenarios. We talked about immigrants crossing the U.S.-Mexico border in enclosed thirteen-wheeler trucks. We talked about people in need arriving at our shores in Florida. I used the glimpse that this exercise offered them to try and open their eyes widely. Figure 4–8 presents a chart outlining a possible experiential approach to teaching *Incidents in the Life of a Slave Girl* specifically by focusing on the senses.

Not all units of study will incorporate all five senses. In some units you can use sight and sound or sight, sound, and feel, for example. The goal should be to

TEXT	SIGHT	SOUND	TASTE	TOUCH	SMELL
Incidents in the Life of a Slave Girl by Harriet Jacobs (1861)	Use maps of the Underground Railroad, tracing her journey and others'. Watch a documentary or film/clips that demonstrate a journey on the Underground Railroad.	Explore enslaved peoples' narratives (Library of Congress). Contact your local refugee support agency and discuss the possibility of a guest. Incorporate poetry written by Black Americans about issues of slavery.	Consider a day where you explore supplement documents that feature cuisine by Black Americans that have roots in slavery.	Visit a local museum that features content related to this topic. Consider visiting a plantation site near you. (Caution: this depends on your student population and other factors.)	Consider taking a local walk in an area that could have been where the Underground Railroad took place and allow students to see that space (an area with many trees, for example).

Figure 4–8 Experiential Unit Sample: Reading and Discussing Refugees

incorporate as much as possible to create an experiential opportunity for students to comprehend the text beyond words. We want them to empathize, to imagine, and to build ideas for how to transform our society. Figure 4–9 is a chart outlining some ideas for incorporating an experiential strategy with different books across middle and high school.

TEXT	SUGGESTIONS	SENSORIAL TRAITS
The Ear, the Eye and the Arm, Nancy Farmer (1994) *Three siblings undertake a forbidden journey in the year 2194 in Zimbabwe and learn about themselves.* (grades 6–8)	Visit a local museum using recycled materials as an art display. Visit the city/town waste management center. Take a ride, as a class, on the city bus.	Sight Smell Feel
One Crazy Summer, Rita Williams-Garcia (2010) *Three sisters go to visit their mother for the summer and learn about her life as a Black Panther.* (grades 6–8)	Host a poetry open mic where students read poetry by Black Panthers and about Black Power. Watch "The Black Panthers: Vanguard of the Revolution" (Nelson 2016) with a discussion. Consider visiting a historic site or museum related to Black Panthers or the Civil Rights period.	Sight Sound Feel

Figure 4–9 Experiential Strategy Unit Ideas

Experiencing Truth

Something to keep in mind as you're planning is age appropriateness. We should be concerned with presenting information in ways that students can process and with content that does not introduce inappropriate ideas for their development. What I mean is, introducing an idea they may not fully be able to grasp and then, not understanding the point of the lesson, they use their misunderstanding in harmful ways. This is not an opportunity to withhold challenging conversations from young students in the name of innocence. This is an opportunity to think critically about how to engage younger students in these delicate but necessary conversations. There exists much scholarship on this matter and some simple online digging can help you establish some rules for how you discuss these important matters with younger students.

We want students to actually learn and retain information. We want them to gain skills that they'll use to tackle the content but also use in their lives. Using our bodies helps us to retain, to learn, to remember. We have to be strategic with what part and details of the content and skills we transform into a physical exercise. What is the most important thing we want to make sure they take away? What skill is that connected to? Crafting this is hard work for us teachers, and that's why it makes a big difference.

CAUTIONS AND CHALLENGES

Challenge:
I did the thing I wasn't supposed to do and created an offensive simulation.

Whew! Take a moment to pause. Owning your mistake is going to be very important here. First, I'd push you to reflect, moment by moment, and step by step, so you can identify all the things you did incorrectly. Then, I'd encourage you to sit with your administrator (if it's at that level) and, in full transparency, share those conclusions and what your next steps are. Receive the feedback. You should then sit with students and share with them what you did that was wrong and how you plan on rectifying it. Usually, that means clarifying misconceptions and correcting wrong information that was learned. Lastly, you should refrain from doing other re-creations until you get a better grasp of the difference between re-creations and simulations and how to plan one effectively.

Challenge:
This feels overwhelming and like it would require a ton of overplanning and extra workload for me.

Sometimes less is more. I don't want you to overplan and burn out. Don't do something performative so you can check a box. Think about the unit you're teaching and which one of the senses you could really hone into. Which one of the senses makes the most sense and will have the deepest learning impact? Which one of the senses will leave a lasting impression on your students?

Adding a Layer of Texture

Teachers who are from the community in which they teach have a big advantage here. I would encourage you to tap in to the people and places that make your community glow. Where can you go and simply read with the class to build rapport? Who in your community has some type of connection to the text you're reading and might be open to coming to talk to your students for thirty minutes? Is there a local restaurant or business you can visit to help your students feel, hear, or see the text? Use your background knowledge, think out of the box, and shine!

The experiential part of Textured Teaching is a great opportunity to also incorporate the interdisciplinary trait of this approach. As you try to focus on the senses or create an exercise to help engage students with the learning, you can easily bring in other content-area knowledge and blend it all together. Use maps, use math charts, use chemistry experiments, become architects, and build something! There is much opportunity with how you create an experience for students and using content knowledge from other subjects is an excellent way to bring this to life.

TEXTURED TEACHING IS FLEXIBLE

> So that we can think and rethink, so that we can create new visions, I celebrate teaching that enables transgressions—a movement against and beyond boundaries. It is that movement which makes education the practice of freedom.
>
> —bell hooks, *Teaching to Transgress*

We often believe that strictness and rules are some of the characteristics of "good teaching." Although structure is important, it often leads to rigidity. Flexibility is essential to facilitate learning as students take more ownership in their learning and are fully engaged. In fact, balance between structure and flexibility is necessary. When I think about professional development I have attended, I get frustrated by my lack of choice in what is taught to me. When a training session does not reflect what I'm doing in my classroom, the needs of my students, or what is happening around us, I become disengaged. Similarly, students will be more engaged when they are involved in what is taught and how they learn.

Educators can center student choice and voice through flexibility and openness. And, because love is a part of Textured Teaching, when we allow students to experience our flexibility, we demonstrate care and compassion. There's a responsiveness embedded in meeting the needs of young people.

Typically, English units involve students answering essential questions, completing a vocabulary word study, reading a novel, doing some grammar exercises, and writing an essay. That's the expected routine. Many teachers experienced this routine as students in English language arts (ELA) or literary studies, and many today practice it in their classrooms. However, it's important to assess students in various ways to see a range of evidence of their abilities to apply their understanding. In *Understanding by Design*, Grant Wiggins and Jay McTighe (2005) have articulated that the six facets of understanding are students being able to explain, being able to interpret, being able to apply, being able to develop perspective, being able to empathize, and having self-awareness (84). Understanding is multilayered, as we can see. Understanding is both intellectual and interpersonal. It is both mind and heart work. Although American society values objectivity and a sense of "academic distance," as Bryan Stevenson (2014), author of *Just Mercy*, says, we also need proximity. It's that proximity that connects clearly with the ideas of literature as either a mirror, window, or sliding glass doors (Sims Bishop 1990). Literature is one of the tools for offering students a form of proximity that will enable and enhance understanding. A failure to understand can lead to bias and lacking multiple points of view.

> *What is the routine in your classroom? Is it like the one outlined here? What feelings come up when you think about changing it?*

Textured Teaching requires applying flexibility to your lesson, unit, and approach to adjust for the students sitting in front of you. A teacher's flexibility makes space for students' humanity and needs. To get started, identify areas in your teaching where you can be more adaptive. This chapter identifies five ways to practice flexibility (see Figure 5–1).

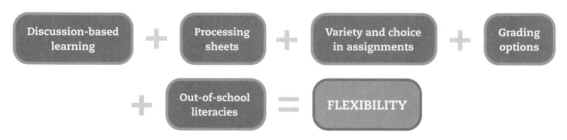

Figure 5–1 A Formula for Flexibility

Strategizing for Flexibility

Strategy #1: Being Flexible with Discussions

Through Textured Teaching you can create multiple opportunities for students to work individually, with a partner, and in small groups, in addition to working as a whole class—often within the same class period. Student talking is a form of thinking and processing and should be heard in a Textured Teaching classroom. In a completely silent classroom where you can always hear a pin drop, students are not practicing group discussion skills or developing healthy communication and work balance habits. Of course there are moments for quiet work time and moments where students are listening to your direct instruction, but there should be a lot of talking outside of that. We want our students to be so engaged in the material that they are overwhelmed with the urge to share their thoughts with partners. Let the kids discuss!

The demystifying and destigmatizing phase described in Chapter 3 is a great moment for structured discussion. There are many discussion strategies you can implement that work well for Textured Teaching. For example, Think, Pair, Share is a well-known process that can be very effective. First, students take a moment to think on their own, then turn to their partner and discuss their ideas, and lastly share with the whole group. This structure allows students to practice sharing their thinking and participating in the larger class discussion. It's also a moment where students can build on each other's work, confer with one another, collaborate, and synthesize learning.

Another strategy, Rotating Leader, engages all the students in the room and elicits critical dialogue about challenging topics. Preselect small groups of four or five students before class starts to strategically take advantage of students' strengths. You would also select four or five leaders. Here's the catch: the leaders are the quietest students in the class, the ones who hesitate to participate in discussions or speak aloud but are strong listeners. Their role in this is to lead the discussions by asking questions and taking notes of the groups' responses. You provide a list of questions. Once each leader takes a seat with a group, round 1 begins. The leader states the question or series of questions and begins taking notes of what the group is sharing. They're just catching main points to create a summary. When the time ends, the leader moves on to the next group. Repeat the same process for a few rounds. The Rotating Leader discussion is finished when each group has seen each leader and answered the different questions. Often, I allot half a class period for this exercise and I offer about ten minutes per round. I may do three rounds, giving thirty minutes for the discussion. Next, each leader is given time (about five to ten minutes) to summarize their notes and select what lines/comments they think are the most poignant. Once they are ready, each leader shares the ideas with the whole class. Through this activity, you've offered students who are rarely noticed during group discussions a moment to shine in a special way. I've used this strategy as a way to debrief an entire unit. After all of the literary analysis has happened and we've completed various tasks, I might use this exercise as a debrief process for students. It can also be used at the halfway mark of a unit to process, to prepare for a quiz, as a formative check-in, and more. This exercise requires movement in a structured manner and openness from you because it can look quite messy and busy.

Jennifer Gonzalez posted a list of discussion strategies on her blog (Gonzalez 2015), two of which I really like. Philosophical Chairs could be an excellent way to discuss topics that are new to students and/or topics that surface many feelings. In these exercises, students select one of two responses: agree or disagree. Based on their selection they sit in a particular chair. Another version of this exercise involves students moving from one side of the room to the other, based on their response. This exercise allows the group to have a visual representation of the ideologies in the room. One of the great opportunities here is to make space for students to share why they've chosen the side they have. After each round where students take a stand or seat, each side gets to share their point of view. If students hear something that resonates with them and they want to switch sides, I welcome that. Help students see how respectful sharing of opinions can impact others.

> **Gallery Walk Guided Questions for Discussion**
>
> *With your partner use these questions to guide your discussion based on your peers' work.*
>
> 1. What general observations can you make about the student's work?
> 2. What claim is this literary analysis making about the text?
> 3. Is the literary analysis clear? If so, what analysis is this work exposing? If not, what is confusing or missing?
> 4. What is the strongest aspect of this work?
> 5. What is an area of development for this work?
> 6. Would you consider this work effective? Why or why not? Cite details that make it effective or ineffective.

Figure 5–2 Gallery Walk Guided Questions for Discussion

Another class discussion activity that I love and I know my students have enjoyed is a Gallery Walk. This is an activity you can host when the end-of-unit student work or projects are completed. There are many ideas about how to do a Gallery Walk. One way that I've done it is as a form of discussion by pairing students and handing them prompts or an evaluation document. As a pair, they walk around and observe their peers' work. They can discuss the products in response to guided questions you provide (Figures 5–2 and 5–3), or they can evaluate the products using the assignment

Gallery Walk Template for Discussion

With your partner, fill out this table as you walk around.

Student	General observations about their work	Questions their work inspires for you	Strongest aspect of their work
Juana	The mask she created meets the skill we were working on. She has a paragraph explaining what she did and that was helpful for me to understand. There is a lot of detail on that mask and it must have taken a very long time.	How long did this mask take to make? Why did you choose that symbol to represent the main character? Do you think the main character was overall good or bad?	The presentation is the strongest part. Juana made the mask look beautiful but also shared so much detail about the character. This was great!

Figure 5–3 Gallery Walk Template for Discussion

rubric. I find that, after Gallery Walks, students are very engaged during presentations because they have already taken the time to think up specific questions and feedback for their peers.

Strategy #2: Being Flexible with Processing Sheets

Another method to incorporate discussion is strategically using what I like to call processing sheets. These are a type of worksheet that I've created a bit of a system for. Also, the word *worksheet* has a generally negative stigma and many folks cringe at the idea. They are often looked down upon by teachers, and rightfully so, because they are typically assigned as busywork for students. *Busywork* is a phrase used to describe rote and mindless classwork that is easily completed, and as a result has low educational impact, but keeps students busy for a period of time. A more productive approach is using processing sheets. These sheets have a few components: text-based evidence questions, comprehension questions, reflection questions, and questions focused on social issues present in the text. Depending on the book, the unit, and the work you're doing, your processing sheet might feature all of the above. I do that often.

Text-based evidence questions are those that require students to dig into the text and find lines or quotes that demonstrate their reasoning. For example, these are prompts that ask why or open-ended questions versus prompts that ask when or closed questions. Questions that ask about character motivation, the impact of literary techniques, turning points in the plot, and more require students to seek in the text and pull out answers. These exercises lead students to defend their ideas, reread the text, and analyze, which moves them beyond comprehension. Comprehension questions are also important, though, because with complex texts we want to make sure students are following along and catching the work the author has laid out for them. Reflection questions are an opportunity for students to make text-to-self connections. Those questions (Figure 5–4) push students to embed themselves in the story.

Lastly, focusing on social issues present in the text can be quite challenging. I have found a way to do this that feels manageable! Learning for Justice has a series of social justice standards available for educators on their website (2018). These standards are arranged in four domains. Each domain focuses on an element of teaching for and about social justice. The first domain is Identity, which teachers can use to help

LEARNING FOR JUSTICE STANDARD	QUESTION OR PROMPT	BOOK USED	GRADE LEVEL
Students will recognize traits of the dominant culture, their home culture, and other cultures and understand how they negotiate their own identity in multiple spaces. (Identity 5)	How does Waheed show traits of the dominant U.S. culture and her ethnic culture throughout her poetry?	*Salt,* Nayyirah Waheed (2013)	9–12
Students will examine diversity in social, cultural, political, and historical contexts rather than in ways that are superficial or oversimplified. (Diversity 10)	Describe how the social and cultural context of the time influences the characters' beliefs about gender roles.	*Blood Wedding,* Federico García Lorca (1993)	11–12
Students will recognize that people's multiple identities interact and create unique and complex individuals. (Identity 3)	Cite examples where Toni Morrison's characterization techniques demonstrate complex individuals.	*The Bluest Eye,* Toni Morrison (1993)	11–12

Reprinted with permission of Learning for Justice, a project of the Southern Poverty Law Center.

Figure 5–4 Learning for Justice Standards' Text-Based Social Issues Questions

students explore their identity, develop language around it, and embrace it without doing so at the expense of others. The second domain is Diversity, which can be used to help students understand the identity of others, celebrate and embrace diversity, and develop accurate language to talk about it. The third domain is Justice and in this area of study, students can explore the idea that there are systems that interact to create inequity and injustice. The fourth domain is Action, and the standards in that domain help teachers to guide students to taking action against injustice. Using those domains as a framework for unit design is a useful tool. I have found that the Identity and Diversity domains are a great opportunity for us ELA teachers to use as a framework for designing our prompts. Sometimes the prompts use the language from the standards directly, and other times the prompt is loosely based on the ideas presented in the standard. Figure 5-4 demonstrates examples of prompts that can be used for specific books based on the standards. Generally speaking, you can take the standard and turn it into a question or you can take the standard and build on an idea presented and create a question.

Differentiated processing sheets can be highly effective and deeply engaging. For example, assembling student groups based on how well they've completed particular tasks, so that you can arrange students in particular combinations, enables you to spread your attention and support to those who might need it a bit more. You can group students based on skills that need to be reassessed or skills that need more practice. Or you can create strategic groupings of students who can be leaders with others who can benefit from their leadership. Be sure that the leaders are able to step away from that group at some point during the class block. I'm sensitive about expecting students to teach other students in my place. Teaching is my job and I don't want to place those expectations on students. That happened to me as a student, and I remember how cumbersome and unfair it felt. Additionally, in my experience, both as a teacher and student, I've noticed it is often the same female students who are assigned this role and that becomes an example of gender-based inequity in the classroom. I love offering leadership opportunities, but unless a student insists, I usually shift groups by the end of that period to release them from that position.

The processing sheets should be engaging and require students to think critically. Imagine processing sheets as a replacement for a written assignment. I typically use large paper, or sheets sized 11 × 17 inches. This helps students see the expectation that there will be lengthy writing, group thinking, deep processing, and that this should take time. Figures 5-5, 5-6, and 5-7 are sample processing sheets. You're welcome to use them as well, but as I mentioned, it is important to individualize these sheets based on your specific class and context.

The processing sheet in Figure 5-5 can be used with sixth and seventh graders to analyze characterization in *Ghost* by Jason Reynolds (2016). Students can work together to complete this work. There are three columns, one for each key character: Ghost, Mom, and Coach. Each column requires students to think about appearance,

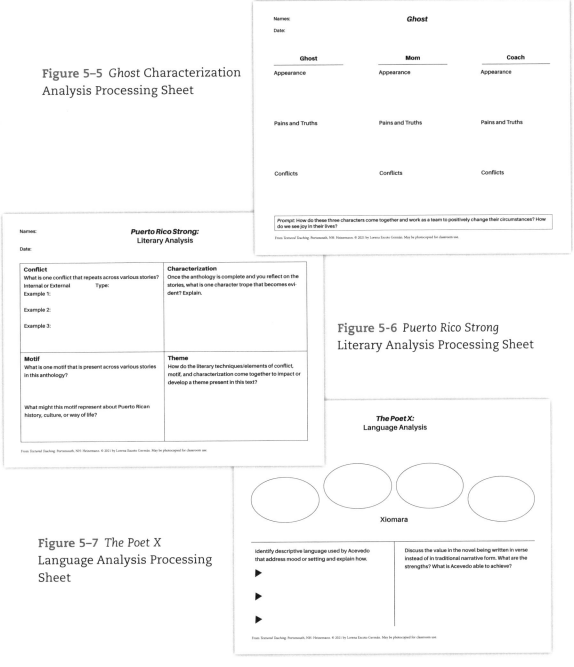

Figure 5–5 *Ghost* Characterization Analysis Processing Sheet

Figure 5-6 *Puerto Rico Strong* Literary Analysis Processing Sheet

Figure 5–7 *The Poet X* Language Analysis Processing Sheet

Blank templates for these three processing sheets can be downloaded at http://hein.pub/TexturedTeaching. Click on Companion Resources.

pains and truths, and conflicts. Pains and truths is a section that is critical for understanding this book, that I may not include on documents for other books. Reynolds created deliberately complex characters that go beyond superficial or stereotypical portrayals of a dysfunctional Black family. I wanted to be sure students saw and analyzed that. The bottom half of the processing sheet is dedicated to seeing joy in the midst of characters' struggles, a necessary aspect of Culturally Sustaining Pedagogy. Casey Wong and Courtney Peña explain in *Culturally Sustaining Pedagogies* (Paris and Alim 2017) how literature is too often focused on our pain without equally centering joy. They ask that in our work to push students toward liberation, we must equally address pain and joy (131). We need students (particularly White ones) to see communities of color living in and experiencing joy. It's part of the resistance. It's how our communities have endured and will continue to survive.

The sheet in Figure 5–6 can be used to analyze various literary techniques in the graphic anthology *Puerto Rico Strong* (Newlevant and Rodriguez 2018). The analysis required is more complex and might therefore be better suited for high schoolers. The page is sectioned into four boxes, and each box focuses on a different literary technique requiring students to read closely, while exploring the voice of a people group oppressed by the United States. One box focuses on conflict in the text and allows for the voice of the Puerto Rican people to shine through. Students search the text to determine what Puerto Ricans identify as their problems, instead of students making that decision for them. The characterization box emphasizes the diversity of the Puerto Rican people and allows students to get to know a Puerto Rican trope. The motif box guides students to synthesize their analysis and think about Puerto Rican way of life, in general. Additionally, using this or another anthology as a whole-class study challenges the notion that in ELA classrooms we only study traditional novels. It doesn't have to be that way. You can advocate for these changes. We have to be ready to claim and model the power we believe our students have.

Lastly, Figure 5–7 is a processing sheet you can use to analyze language in Elizabeth Acevedo's *The Poet X* (2018) with high schoolers. The top part of the document asks students to identify words that Xiomara, the main character, uses to describe herself. In a society where the dominant culture often gets to name and characterize the rest of the cultures, we're making space for a woman of color—an Afro Caribeña—to powerfully name and describe herself. We're listening and taking notes! The bottom left corner legitimizes Acevedo's voice as a writer by pushing students to search directly in the text for exemplary writing. The bottom right of the sheet continues this idea by focusing on the power and effectiveness of novels in verse. Using a young adult novel in verse to study language and literary techniques is revolutionary, considering what low opinions many ELA teachers hold of the value and potential of young adult literature.

Strategy #3: Being Flexible with Out-of-School Literacies

As discussed earlier, our students leave our classrooms and engage in literacy activities daily. Whether they are reading novels, reading statuses on Instagram, writing rap lyrics, texting constantly, singing songs, and/or speaking other languages, they are engaged in highly literate activities outside of school. How can we welcome those activities and offer students ways to get "credit" for learning? There are college courses that require students to discuss the course matter online. Our students might not be on Instagram creating stories about the book you're reading, but what they are posting or seeing others post might have direct connections to the topics you're discussing in class. So, how do you know what they're doing outside of school hours? Relationship. It's important to build rapport for these reasons (and more). Make it a point to spend time daily or weekly chatting and socializing with students, either individually or in small groups. Get to know what's going on in their social scene and what students are doing outside of school. Identify material that they can bring in to class, and find ways to incorporate it into the lessons. Class journals are also a good tool for this. In the past I had students write in a journal that stayed in our class. I was able to read through them and respond. That back-and-forth in their journals is a great place to listen to what's going on in their lives and help them make direct connections with the class content. Dr. Tim San Pedro, professor at The Ohio State University, explains in Chapter 6 of *Culturally Sustaining Pedagogies* (Paris and Alim 2017) that "in such a move to re-center students' experiences that may counter standard curricula, students who were once marginalized by monocultural and monolingual curricula can begin to reinvest in their education because they can see themselves and their stories" (113).

San Pedro's point leads me to think about another group of students that greatly benefit from welcoming out-of-school literacies and that's immigrant students who are people of color. These students are often coming to the United States and facing terribly deficit perspectives about who they are and what they can do. Yet, research and lived experiences show us that these young people are multitaskers, highly talented, hardworking, and living lives overflowing with literacies. Welcoming what they do outside of our classrooms would be a great way to celebrate them, welcome their cultures, and show them that they belong.

How can you integrate that extracurricular literacy into class content? Flexibility. You need to make space and room for the unplanned and unexpected treasure finds.

Have you ever welcomed an extracurricular text as part of a classroom discussion? What are some questions you can use to inspire students to search for connections?

On one occasion, during a conversation with a student named Dulce, I learned she had started writing poetry at home. I invited her to share some of it with me. She was surprised I was interested, but very excited and willing to share. As I sat in my chair, reading through her notebook, I identified one poem that directly connected to the protagonist of our text! I asked, actually begged, Dulce to allow me to share her poem. She acquiesced, but only if I did it anonymously. When I made copies and shared the poem with the class, we discussed its literary merit and made connections to the text. Students felt they could relate to the poem and were boasting about how true and valuable it was. I remember my conversation with Dulce after school that day. She was in awe that her poetry could inspire so many, that it touched their lives, that they made connections to a published author, and that they had liked it. On another occasion, I had a student named Roberto share a tattoo on his arm. From his point of view, his tattoo was a visual representation of a theme present in our class novel. Roberto told us the story behind it and its meaning in his life. Welcoming a tattoo, or other types of writing, allows students to see the literacy in their everyday lives that they may have not even considered before. Additionally, including these extracurricular literacies opens their minds to what can be read in a class and what can be studied. It blurs the line between the classroom and the outside world and allows the two to merge, creating socially conscious researchers and students.

The flexibility of making space for our students' personal lives in a way that honors their stories leads to complexity and texture. Our classes become spaces for depth, honesty, and heartfelt experiences. Truth, justice, and love help build community. These experiences impact our students and us, as teachers. When we think about how schooling has historically operated in the United States, and we take on Textured Teaching, we are creating restorative spaces for students. Modeling flexibility for them is an important lifelong lesson. Hopefully, as they engage in the world around them, they will respond with patience and flexibility. Navigating challenging and tense situations while keeping our sense of purpose is a necessary part of life. That's how we endure in teaching and that's what we model in the classroom when we're flexible. When we do it with grace, love, and justice in mind, we make way for real change. Our classrooms become physical areas where students can heal from oppression and imagine a better future for all of us.

Regardless of your student demographic, all students should be doing this work. It benefits White students by allowing them to hear voices different from their own, but also it presents them with complex and often unheard perspectives and points of view. It goes beyond the superficial representations often presented about people of color. Students of color will benefit from this by hearing their grandmothers, their mothers, their uncles, their fathers, and themselves in these stories. They'll be able to rest on their own lived experiences to complete the work and participate in academic study. That is an affirming experience I wish I'd had.

Strategy #4: Being Flexible with Assessments

There are a variety of tools students can use to demonstrate both comprehension and literary analysis. In your Textured Teaching classroom, students should be able to use creativity when demonstrating what they've learned. The five-paragraph essay has its uses; however, it is not the pinnacle of academic rigor. If you use the essay format, make sure that students understand that prioritizing the written word and the five-paragraph essay is limiting and grounded in bias. How students are assessed should lead to a demonstration of skill mastery, not just a completion of tasks. Students may easily complete a worksheet, finish a text, or complete a written response and not have mastered the skills you've been working on.

Teachers can create a great opportunity for students to take ownership of their educational experience by incorporating student voice in what is taught, how it is taught, and how learning is demonstrated. It prepares students to be independent learners and critical thinkers and to practice metacognitive skills in a real-life scenario: their grades. The following are some tips for ways to be flexible with assessments.

Tip: Try Creative Analysis Projects

This is a literary analysis assessment that pushes students to go beyond the written word to creatively demonstrate their thinking. It is important to not place a heavy focus on aesthetics per se. If a student is not artistically inclined, they should still be able to do this assignment in a way that is exemplary. Artistic skills are not a requirement; creating a representation of your thinking is. Figure 5–8 displays how to create an assignment based on specific academic skills.

The student products can take many shapes and formats. Figure 5–9 shows a creative analysis, in this case, a representation of the student's response to building background for *Gabi, a Girl in Pieces* by Quintero (2014). Students were tasked with exploring how they self-identify and shared with the class a brief oral rationale for their

ACADEMIC SKILL	ASSIGNMENT
Identify an important literary element in the text and demonstrate how it impacts the development of the story. (grades 9–12)	Create a representation of your analysis where you include two textual items: the name of the element you are analyzing and the best quote that highlights this element. You can use imagery inspired from the text in your analysis. Fit it into a paper that is $8\frac{1}{2}$ by 11 inches.
Analyze the author's use of word choice through a close reading of a section of the text. (grades 9–12)	Using large paper, re-create the text you are closely reading, and as if it were a Google Doc, add "comments," images, and anything else you can think of to accurately analyze the author's word choice.
Analyze the characterization developed by the author. (grade 6)	Create a mask that best describes aspects of your selected character. Somewhere on the mask include a representation of the character's growth process.

Figure 5–8 Sample Assignments with Skill Focus

Figure 5–9 Self-Identity Representation

choices. In her product, this student features a hand at the center of her work, representative of her and her presence, surrounded by fire due to the intensity of her culture and conflict within herself because of her biracial and bicultural identity. She also included writing that she selected from some of her reflections, completed before this assignment. Figure 5-10 goes a bit deeper with a piece analyzing plot and conflict in

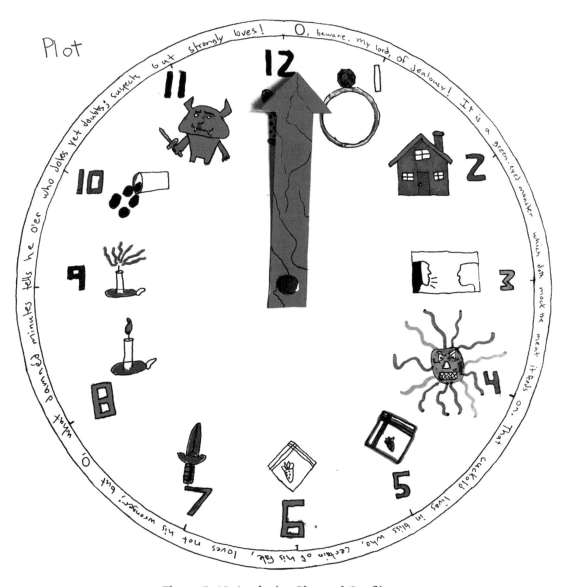

Figure 5–10 Analyzing Plot and Conflict

Shakespeare's *Othello*. The student was concerned with visualizing the way the story moved and flowed while also considering how conflict was related to that development. He represented his thinking by creating a clock and using symbolism to express his ideas. This was a multilayered representation of his thinking and quite an example of critical thinking, to say the least.

As a teacher, you can be empowered beside your students to engage them in texts and analyses that are complex, invite critical thinking, and permit flexibility through tasks, projects, and assessments. When students showcase their work, they have a chance to feel proud and affirmed among peers. In the process of it all, the text comes alive through Textured Teaching.

Tip: Try Extended Responses

As you continue to provide students with options, you can incorporate written assignments that are longer than a paragraph, but shorter than a five-paragraph essay—what I call extended responses. This is a three-paragraph essay without the drawn-out introduction and conclusion. These written tasks focus on analysis and organization. Can students develop several solid paragraphs of deep and critical literary analysis and organize their points well? As an added bonus, this eliminates a common hurdle for students writing an introduction: writer's block. Although they still produce one or two introductory sentences that are brief and purpose driven, the goal is to spend more time on the analysis and argument development. The resulting three paragraphs can be quite lengthy. They should include citations from the text and the typical elements of a literary analysis. What's the point of this? Diversity in choice and flexibility for students.

Tip: Try Assessments in Which Students Choose the Skill and/or Product

To laser focus on elements in the text, create assessments that are focused on the text you've read in class and are deeply analytical and highly rigorous. Start by determining a few main skills you want to assess. Then, offer students a choice for how they demonstrate mastery. Next, the assessment design process begins. These require in-class discussion, preparation time, planning, and conferring with you. Together, you determine what might be the best way for the student to demonstrate that skill. You'll be surprised by how impressive their ideas are and how much academic risk they take when the choice is theirs.

Students are rarely presented with this flexibility to design their own assessments. This freedom will be inspiring to some and overwhelming for others. One way to meet students where they are is to offer a menu of options. You can create lists of assessment ideas based on the skill(s) you're addressing, or you can use an "assessment bingo" chart like the one shown in Figure 5–11. Above the chart, you'll see a list of the skills addressed by the assessment. Communicating what skills they're working on allows students to be cognizant of what they're doing and helps them with vision and purpose. The chart can be used by asking students to select an item from each of the columns, which address the skills stated above the chart. For example, column one, on the left, addresses the first stated skill: identify and analyze a literary element present in the text. The second column in the center addresses the second skill about how the element impacts the novel as a whole, and the last column on the right addresses the third skill listed at the top about how these literary elements interact. If a student were to select 1, 5, and 9, for example, by drawing a line diagonally across the chart, they would have a comprehensive analysis of the text. They would produce a close reading of the setting, create a web association map about how setting impacts the novel as a whole, and then take their analysis deeper by talking about the relationship between setting and symbolism through photography. Regardless of the direction in which you go, the students will produce highly critical and rigorous course work. These assessments can be adapted to any grade level. In my experience, as students approach middle school, the more metacognition that takes place in their learning process, the better performance they tend to display.

Strategy #5: Being Flexible with Grading

You may have wondered how to grade the assignments mentioned previously. In the same way texture is present in your design, texture is present in your grading. Your grading should be based on mastery of the skills you're addressing. Oftentimes grading feels highly subjective, and students question us about grades. Although students should feel comfortable questioning us and asking about their grades, grading should be a transparent process and expectations should be clear from the beginning. That leads students to feel like learning is a partnership, and hopefully they'll carry those expectations with them outside of our classrooms, too.

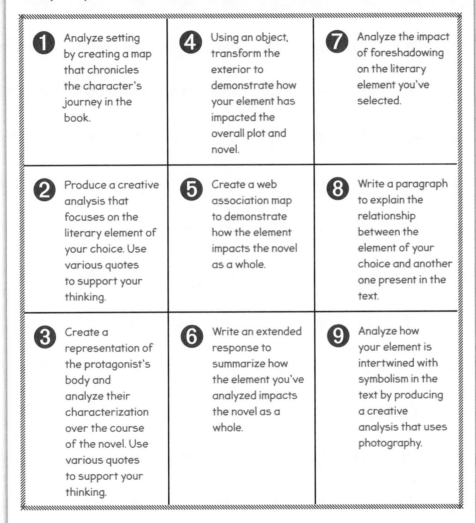

Assessment Bingo

Identify and analyze a literary element present in the text.
Explain how that element impacts the novel as a whole.
Briefly analyze how that element interacts with another element.

1 Analyze setting by creating a map that chronicles the character's journey in the book.

4 Using an object, transform the exterior to demonstrate how your element has impacted the overall plot and novel.

7 Analyze the impact of foreshadowing on the literary element you've selected.

2 Produce a creative analysis that focuses on the literary element of your choice. Use various quotes to support your thinking.

5 Create a web association map to demonstrate how the element impacts the novel as a whole.

8 Write a paragraph to explain the relationship between the element of your choice and another one present in the text.

3 Create a representation of the protagonist's body and analyze their characterization over the course of the novel. Use various quotes to support your thinking.

6 Write an extended response to summarize how the element you've analyzed impacts the novel as a whole.

9 Analyze how your element is intertwined with symbolism in the text by producing a creative analysis that uses photography.

Figure 5–11 Assessment Bingo Chart Sample

Tip: Try Cocreating Rubrics

Typically, teachers create or use a precreated rubric and apply grades to student work. I know I've done that, myself. However, this often leaves students asking questions about their grades, especially when they disagree. What if students played a role in creating those rubrics? Two ways of being flexible with rubrics are cocreating a class rubric with students and creating a student-specific rubric. Your choice will depend on how the unit is designed. For example, if students have the freedom to select their own skills from a list, then you may need to offer individual rubrics. If the whole class is working on the same skill, then together you can cocreate a rubric. You would typically codesign a rubric with your students once the assignment has been shared and students are clear about the task at hand. This might be toward the middle or end of the unit, after the reading and many discussions are completed. Start by sharing the skill set or the standards with the whole class. As a group, discuss them and ensure comprehension. Once that is clear, as a group you determine what performance does not meet the skill and what performance does meet the skill. If this isn't a way to teach them how to lead themselves, how to build together, and how to change the world collectively, I don't know what is.

> *Have you ever considered cocreating a rubric with your students? How do you think it would impact the power dynamic between you and the students? What would you have to change or adjust in your approach?*

Figure 5–12 shows a rubric I cocreated with one of my sixth-grade classes for an assessment on characterization. The task involved creating a mask that analyzed the author's development of a character in the story. After discussing the skills we would be working on, we brainstormed what an effective mask should look like. I found that students were fully capable of having this conversation, and they knew what an effective product should contain. I also observed that once they were clear on the expectations, they generally met them and some exceeded them. They took ownership of their work and overall, the masks were of high quality.

When it was time to grade the student work, using this rubric was helpful. You can use a rubric like this one in two ways. First, you can offer points for each column and use that total to determine if the work is effective or ineffective, thus necessitating that the student develop their work further and resubmit. Second, you can skip the number grade/points system and simply grade as effective or ineffective, which is a strategy I think works best with student discussion.

The Mask		
	Effective	**Ineffective**
Appearance • Detail • Effort • Functionality	Mask is neat, stays on, and demonstrates attention to detail. The detail focuses on the characterization and can be linked to moments in the story.	Mask is sloppy, disorganized, falls off, and does not demonstrate attention to detail. It doesn't impact the audience.
Analysis • Symbolism • Resemblance to character • Visual representation of thinking	Mask is thoughtful, has color and objects that demonstrate analysis and symbolism. It is clear who the character is and how they're being analyzed.	Mask is not put together well, has minimal objects or colors that symbolize the character. The character's identity is not clear.

Figure 5–12 Sample Cocreated Rubric (Grade 6)

Tip: Grading Discussions in Various Ways

Many English teachers use Socratic discussions or concentric circles (Gonzalez 2015). Regardless of the structure you choose for discussions, how you grade matters as a Textured Teacher. One way to grade students is by granting credit for multiple forms of participation. Figure 5-13 shows a table I've used for grades and feedback during discussions. Each column has a purpose and students are fully aware of what is expected. The second column, labeled "Analytical Contribution," is space where you can note student analytical contributions. These include citations from the text, new ideas, references to literary devices, and more. The third column, labeled "Building Contribution," is one where you can recognize students who echo others by building on their ideas. They might add another literary citation as an example, or relate it to a previous point, and more. In the fourth column, labeled "Challenging Contribution," you can recognize students who disagree or refute a point. They might critique an idea by presenting a counterpoint. The final column allows us teachers a way to "see" all the students during discussion. On some occasions, I noted how a student, Malika, took notes during the entire discussion even though they didn't participate. Based on Malika's linguistic development, I offered them a chance to summarize and contribute their own analysis privately, at a later time.

Student	Grading Area			
	Analytical Contribution	**Building Contribution**	**Challenging Contribution**	**Comment**
Ambar	Surfaced how the main charac-ter was strug-gling with an internal conflict in Chapters 1–3. He read two quotes to support his idea. He says plot is impacted by the main character's internal conflict.	Supported Melissa's point about tension in Chapter 4 with his own example.		Noticed he took notes and high-lighted his text when peers noted lines/moments he had not noticed. Highly engaged throughout the discussion. Awesome work!
Jose Luis		Supported another student's point about the tone of the text and cited addi-tional evidence (Chapters 2 and 6).	Countered the idea that the main character was not abusive by citing evidence of his abusive language toward women in the text.	Seemed to check out during the end of the dialogue. Follow up next class.

Figure 5–13 Grading Table

Creating differentiated opportunities for students to contribute in their own unique ways during class discussions is practicing sensitivity and care, which is a way to love in action. Responding to the students in front of you, and meeting them where they are, is simply good teaching. We've always had students in our classes with unique needs, but I'm not sure we've always been openly having conversations about that. Today, there are more and more students with learning challenges and who have dif-ferent needs for learning. One of the biggest challenges this presents for us is how to meet the needs of so many different people through the same content. The real answer is that our current general approach to education doesn't allow us to. But what I have learned is that through Textured Teaching and, particularly, being flexible with assessments, there are some major gains and wins for students.

Students who have dyslexia, for example, have amazing strengths in so many areas. Although handwriting may not be one of them, many of these students are very good listeners and visual thinkers and have strong spatial skills. Students with dysgraphia also have struggles when it comes to handwriting, but in their case, they are also often blessed with strong visual and spatial skills. Why not offer them opportunities to use their strengths to demonstrate their learning and mastery of skills? Why assess them in a way where the assessment itself is the barrier? This is the case when we don't offer a variety of assessments or choice in assessments: we leave some students behind (pun intended) and we don't truly know what they've actually learned. On the other hand, it has been my experience that when we are open-minded and allow space for students with differences to shine in our class-rooms, it builds relationships with them and their parents. These students feel seen and believe they can actually succeed—often for the first time. Don't we do better when we feel acknowledged and supported as teachers? Of course we do! In Figure 5–14 I show how these assessments offer opportunities for students with common learning challenges.

Oftentimes an argument raised against what I'm articulating here is that students need to perform according to the "normal requirements" in the "real world" and when they get a job. My answer to this is that there are so many new jobs out there today that didn't exist before and there are so many skill sets we teach that are in fact useless considering the advancements of technology. I'm not saying I don't value those skill sets; I'm saying we can't force others to value them, and we have to make space for students to succeed. Through flexible assessments I think we serve all of our students better. It's equitable. Additionally, overprioritizing skills to the detriment of identity development, antibias and antiracist understanding, and critical skills is harmful to the long-term project of positive social transformation (Muhammad 2019, 86). Even the teachers that believe themselves to be apolitical and just want to promote civic engagement or kindness can agree that students need to engage with society in a respectful and peace-making manner. As Textured Teachers, we know that kindness and skills are not enough. It's led us to where we are today.

ASSESSMENT STRATEGY	LEARNING CHALLENGE THAT IT SUPPORTS	HOW IT SUPPORTS STUDENTS
Discussion-based assessments	Dyslexia, dysgraphia	Students can participate in waves and might excel at listening to others.
Processing sheets	Dysgraphia	Students can chunk their work, collaborate with others to build on their ideas; doesn't require lengthy writing.
Welcoming out-of-school literacies	Dyslexia, dysgraphia, ADD, ADHD	Whatever students are able to do out of school, in their home/safe spaces can count toward school work.
Extended responses	Dyslexia, dysgraphia	Students are not required to write as much and can focus on the analysis portion of their explanations.
Creative analyses	Dyslexia, dysgraphia, ADD, ADHD	Students can use all their strengths and work at their own pace.
Text-based assessments	Dyslexia, dysgraphia	Students can choose both what skill to focus on and how they'll demonstrate mastery.

Figure 5–14 Assessment Strategies and Learning Challenges

Offering flexibility with assessments was one of the strongest success points I experienced when I worked with emergent bi- and multilingual students in a predominantly immigrant setting. When they came to my class, the expectations as mandated by the state were unrealistic and unsettling, at best. I couldn't expect my students to have all of the English language necessary to analyze what we were talking about or to express their ideas. It would have been inhumane to fail them. By offering alternate ways to express their thinking instead, I was able to build a strong rapport and allowed them to succeed. Creating opportunities for them to demonstrate their analysis left them feeling confident about their abilities and selves. One of the frameworks we can consider when assessing emergent bilinguals is the C6 Biliteracy Instructional Framework (Medina n.d.). It begins by stating what the literacy areas are and the skills students need to work on. Medina states that it's a 4 + 1 step where we focus on speaking, listening, reading, writing, and metalinguistic awareness. That last step is crucial and requires that the teacher have social and cultural competence. Your assessments and tasks can focus on all these skills while meeting students' social emotional needs as you address issues of justice, particularly ones affecting them as immigrants and students of color in the United States. Additionally, the framework provides six actions that are the foundation for the teaching approach: create, connect, collaborate, communicate, consider, and commit. Textured Teaching pairs well with this framework because both argue that our students' identity formation and learning about justice do not replace content learning or skill building. Through this framework, teachers support emergent bilinguals by creating authentic learning experiences, connecting to their home languages, collaborating with them, communicating and modeling language goals, considering their individual needs, and committing to teaching them well and serving them effectively. Textured Teachers do all of this. We are committed to helping emergent bilinguals to develop their literacy skills and use them for the betterment of their lives, their rights, and ultimately, our society.

As you can see, these strategies require flexibility and openness from you. There are moments when there will be chatter, when students will be independent from you, when students will be moving around and shifting from corner to corner, but you must trust the process! Students sitting neatly and quietly in rows "doing work" does not mean there is critical thinking—or even learning—occurring. Sometimes teachers believe that what I just described is classroom management, but I see it as body management. It prohibits students from learning in their own ways, and it's fully about the teacher's control. That same preoccupation with control and managing bodies is at the core of White supremacy. When we, as educators and schools, are more concerned

What are some of the values that frame your classroom management approach? Have you ever considered how this approach might be rooted in bias?

about quiet classrooms and still children who comply and obey rather than young people who are learning, expressing themselves, and engaging in experiences that will prepare them to lead, then we are not creating restorative spaces. We are concerned about robot children who do as we say. We are furthering the oppressive system Paris and Alim (2017) are asking us to dismantle. If students ever develop the skills to lead, to change the world, to speak up, to be free, it will have been despite our classrooms, not because of them.

CAUTIONS AND CHALLENGES

Challenge:
Students are frustrated by the challenge of selecting or designing their own assessment.

I've noticed that when students become frustrated, it's less about the task at hand and more that they feel overwhelmed. In response, physically go to them and sit by their side. Start a conversation about their feelings and create space for them to vent. When they're finished, ask them if individual attention from you might help them—that usually helps them to calm down—then tell them that you can restart the assignment together to figure out where they got stumped. Pacing their brainstorming and design process by helping them walk slowly through it all usually helps students feel supported and helps them choose confidently.

Challenge:
Meeting departmental and school requirements

I've worked in schools where I could only choose one text for the entire year. The rest were chosen for me. Even the assessments I assigned were mandated! In such scenarios, your autonomy barely exists, but implementing Textured Teaching in those schools can happen, albeit barely. It requires identifying units or books where you can add an extra week, for example, so you can offer these students an additional activity that becomes one of these assessments. Consider having a colleague join your class for a week so you can finish one of the mandated assessments faster and then create time and space for the Textured Teaching assessment/activity. Think creatively and come up with your own outside-the-box solutions.

Adding a Layer of Texture

The following idea works best for educators who have strong relationships with students and can hold them accountable. Here's the challenge:

- At the start of the unit, share with students that they are going to create an entire unit of study.
- Next, present the class with the learning goals and objectives.
- Do a quick book talk of two to four texts they can choose from for the unit. Explain that those books are good options for meeting the stated learning goals.
- Allow students the chance to collaborate and design how they will use those texts to meet the learning goals.
- Let them know they will also cocreate the rubric as you approach the end of the unit.

This is a great opportunity to de-center yourself and offer students a genuine moment for leadership. They can do a lot of creating while still working within a framework or guidelines. This will offer them some structure, while still offering them choice.

Notes

TEXTURE

> We all have a duty to fight for freedom. It is our duty to win. We must love and support each other. We have nothing to lose but our chains.
>
> —Assata Shakur, *Assata: An Autobiography*

A truth about Textured Teaching is that it comes from a place of frustration and pain inside of me: the pain of having been wronged by educational institutions; the frustration of being silenced, ignored, and neglected. These feelings pushed me into knowing I could do better and believing that the classroom could be different.

If only my teachers would have known how to teach us the skills and language for effective and critical discussion.

If only my teachers would have considered meaningful representation in the texts they chose to teach us.

If only my teachers would have known who we really were.

Did they know that my father's family in the Dominican Republic had been part of the political movement to oust the dictator that terrorized the country for thirty years, or that on my mother's side of the family there were engineers, educators, translators, and seamstresses? No. Nor did they know that my friend Yinka's family came from a long line of educated people in Nigeria or that in Cinthia and Neisha's families there were medical professionals and business owners. Did they assume that this richness could have really been among and within us? Did they believe we had anything to offer? It seems like they didn't. The evidence says they saw us through a stereotypical and deficit lens. They spent our elementary and secondary careers showing us all the ways we were lacking when compared with White heteronormative standards of intelligence and success. We were called minorities, poor, sometimes delinquents, and other dehumanizing and disrespectful labels. They failed to see that we were on our way to becoming teachers, nurses, engineers, doctors, graphic designers, government officials, leaders, and more. Did they know that one day I might be returning to offer them professional development? I guess not. But why not? Because I often heard them describe the young people from neighboring communities as "our future bosses" or "leading me one day." So, it wasn't *only* about adultism. There was more. There's always more.

So much of the Textured Teaching approach is about allowing students the leadership opportunity to drive their own learning and to celebrate and sustain the community in which they live.

This is why Textured Teaching starts with love and is sustained by the values of justice, love and community, and truth and knowledge. That's why implementing it requires being student driven and community centered, using an interdisciplinary approach, maintaining flexibility as a value, and using experiential strategies. I broke it all the way down (I hope) in this book so that we can stop wondering and guessing how social justice is implemented in the classroom. This doesn't have to be a guessing game or a secret. It might be a bit confusing until you get into your groove and adjust your approach to your context, but if social justice or doing the right thing was always easy, it would have been done. It is imperative that we all adopt a Textured Teaching approach and work toward social justice through education together.

So much of the Textured Teaching approach is about allowing students the leadership opportunity to drive their own learning and to celebrate and sustain the community in which they live. If done well, it feels seamless and not like a fad that you are ungenuinely tagging on to the work to feel "relatable." I know there are teachers who add "social justice" units or "community action" projects, but if it isn't embedded in their overall teaching approach, it feels performative, at best. Students can see that performativity a mile away, and we all (students and fellow educators) know the one-off moment in the curriculum will not necessarily carry on throughout the year. The message received is that the teacher sees social justice as just a box to check—something to get over with so they can focus on other things—and doesn't see the way these issues are embedded in all the other topics students will be covering over the year. The pressures of testing, standards, and imposed curriculum are real. We can't ignore that, and yet that might be the fight you and your students take on. Attaching a single book, lesson, or project in your curriculum that finally allows students a chance to practice being themselves and being leaders addressing a social injustice is not the same as it being a lived-in part of your approach. One thing is having a great workout one day and another is integrating wellness thoughtfully and intentionally into your lifestyle. The latter is a lifestyle of self-care. That's the one that will yield results.

Think about Textured Teaching as integrated self-care: What does it mean to welcome the whole humanity of our students into our classrooms? How can we create spaces where they are authentically themselves? What does it look like to shift away from upholding standards created by someone else that only serve to minimize our students? To do this, we have to honor the wholeness of people. We have to see and respect all the elements that inform who we are, including the following:

- ancestors
- beliefs
- languages and home words
- laughter
- anger
- food

- pains
- errors
- successes
- growth
- losses
- multiple definitions of love

We each bring all of that with us when we walk into a room, and so much more. Textured Teaching aspires to allow our students be their full selves in our classrooms. We *can* curate inclusive spaces that inspire this in our students.

A Tool for You: Unit Plan Template

In the first column of the template, document the text you are using, the goal of the unit, and the date range. It is helpful to have a sense of the number of lessons a unit will take as you consider when to incorporate the experiential element and coordinate any guest speakers. I draw my essential questions from Learning for Justice's Social Justice Standards (2018), simply transforming them into questions that I use to guide my discussion with students.

The second column is used to plan the content skills you want to address during that unit. In this template I'm using *Puerto Rico Strong* (Newlevant and Rodriguez 2018), an anthology that provides a good opportunity to task students with making connections across stories.

The third column is where you'll plan for the interdisciplinary elements of the unit. Here, you can identify terms you want to demystify and destigmatize as well concepts to research during your building background and research stage. You can plan the supplements here, as well.

TEXT, ESSENTIAL QUESTION, TIME FRAME	CONTENT SKILLS	INTERDISCIPLINARY ELEMENTS
Puerto Rico Strong (2018) edited by Hazel Newlevant and Desiree Rodriguez How do the various aspects of their identities make Puerto Rican people unique and complex? 4 weeks	Theme Motif Imagery Symbolism	**Demystify**: Latinx African Diaspora Nuyorican Commonwealth **Research topics:** 1. History of Puerto Rico as a commonwealth 2. Los Macheteros 3. Puerto Rican immigration to U.S. 4. Terms: *coqui, Borinquen, Boricua,* and racial makeup of Puerto Rico 5. Hurricane Maria 6. Famous Puerto Ricans **Supplements:** Music/arts—bachata and merengue, national anthem History/law/political science—guest speaker will discuss U.S. relations with Puerto Rico and connected topics Psychology—readings discussing the trauma of surviving hurricanes

Figure 6–1 Sample Unit Plan Template

EXPERIENTIAL ACTIVITY	FLEXIBLE AND STUDENT DRIVEN ASSESSMENT	PROCESS AND COMMUNITY CENTERING
Sound: music analysis of national anthem, guest speakers Sight: Videos of Puerto Rican day parades in New York, Hurricane Maria–related videos	Students will produce a work that explains their analysis of theme and motif in the anthology. Students will choose a format to represent their learning of the experiential activities.	▌ Demystify ▌ Build background and research ▌ Read and use literary circles to process student-selected pages ▌ Supplement and guest speakers

The last column is where you plan out the order of the unit, or the process of learning. Here, you can plan for when you want to bring in guest speakers or where you want to strategically include sensorial activities.

The fifth column is dedicated to how you will assess students and the places where they can drive the learning. This column helps you see how the unit begins to come together. It's often highly effective to know the goals and assessment as you develop the content of the unit.

In the fourth column, list all the ways you will use the senses to reach your students and enhance their analysis and appreciation of the work.

How do you know if you're a Textured Teacher? We (now) agree that each unit should be experiential, flexible, student driven, community centered, and interdisciplinary, but that can be a lot to keep track of! Well, in an effort to synthesize all of what Textured Teaching is and can be, I am offering a unit planning tool that I use to keep all the elements in mind. There is flexibility in how you implement it (of course), but I find that templates help me very much when planning. You can use the template presented in Figure 6–1 to organize your thinking and planning as you develop a unit based on a text. Each column of the template offers a space for you to think about all of the elements of Textured Teaching when constructing your units. Know that you can use the template columns in any order you wish—it might be that after completing the first two columns you want to work on the fifth and plan backward. Be flexible!

A blank unit plan template can be downloaded at http://hein.pub/TexturedTeaching. Click on Companion Resources.

The Texture We Already Have

We must consider the texture we already have. Celebrate it in your own life. How else will you model this for students or be able to celebrate them? Get to know yourself, your textures, your curves, the interwoven fabrics of your life, and bring that into the classroom. When we see the texture in our students, we're better able to make connections to the texts. For example, when teaching *Night* by Elie Weisel (1960) to a group of Dominican and Puerto Rican tenth graders, I noticed my students felt the text was distanced from their lived experiences. I knew the students weren't the issue—I had to make direct connections for them. Before our next class gathering, I moved all the chairs in the room into a circle and brought out a class set of *A Convenient Hatred: The History of Antisemitism* (Goldstein 2011), a great tool for dialogue that demonstrates a pattern of global historic anti-Semitism, through narration of recent history alongside beautiful and harrowing artwork and maps. Once the students entered the classroom and were sitting in their

Get to know yourself, your textures, your curves, the interwoven fabrics of your life, and bring that into the classroom.

seats, I began telling them the story of one of my aunts who lived in the Dominican Republic and worked at the airport where she met many people. One day, she met a Jewish man and although neither spoke each other's language, they fell in love. Years later, they moved to Israel. My Dominican, platano-eating, Spanish-speaking, formerly merengue-dancing aunt was now an Orthodox Jew living in Israel! The students were shocked. When I finished telling the story, they asked questions about life in Israel, and I shared what I had heard from my aunt and other relatives who had more details than I did. We laughed at the audacity of love and the adventure that is life. I then shared that the book *Night* was somewhat personal for me because it allowed me to understand a bit more about the plight of a people group that my own aunt was now a part of. The class grew silent. I turned our attention to the pictures and the maps in the book, and we dove in to better understand the historical context of the Jewish story. They traced the time lines with their fingertips. They closely analyzed the imagery. Sharing a bit of me, sharing my personal connection to this book made all the difference. Being Latinx in the United States means understanding historic oppression and problematic governmental policies. That part was easy for them to relate to. After this one conversation, the students were more engaged. I was able to help them see the opportunity of a connection for them with the content of the book. I also believe that providing them with historical and political context through the use of artwork and time lines, all visual tools, was an important touch. That personal, interdisciplinary, and sensorial approach can be Textured Teaching. This isn't magic. It's an intentional strategy.

Although the classroom isn't about you or centered on you, you are certainly an important member, as is each student. Often, as teachers we remove ourselves so much from the community in our classrooms that the silence of our nonparticipation impedes community building and rapport. Why should students share themselves when we've held back so clearly? So, open up and share, too. Bring a bit of yourself and let them see your texture.

I open up with students by sharing reasons why I select some of the books I do. I tell them short anecdotes from my own schooling and childhood and how that has impacted how I teach. I share a bit about parallels between me and characters. I share voices from my community through units and supplements. When I first began at my current school, I could sense a distance between me and my small group of students—I felt it, physically. In a school that is all about hugs, I rarely even received high fives. I knew I had to share a bit of myself with my students. On the wall of our classroom, I had a large and laminated poster of Tupac Shakur's (1999) poem "The Rose That Grew from Concrete." It's one of my all-time favorite poems for many reasons, one of which is that I can identify with the rose. I decided one Friday to stop our lesson early, interrupt the routine, and get a little personal. We put all of the chairs to the side and cleared an area of the room where we sat on the floor gathered around the poster. First, I read the poem. I asked students to share their initial thoughts and what they thought the poem meant. Then, I had a student read the poem. After the second reading, students had more ideas about the poem, and even more after another student read the poem a third time. After the third reading, I shared what I thought of the poem and opened up a bit about my high school experience. All the students were fully engaged and listening to the stories intently—one young man's jaw dropped in surprise when I talked about gangs and street violence, a life he knew nothing about. I then told my students why I'd put that poem up on the wall: "It's here because it's a reminder that regardless of where I come from—regardless of the concrete that I broke out of—I'm still standing and breathing and walking. It's a reminder that I'm strong. Today, I get to be here with you and share this important piece of writing." I felt a palpable shift. Once I shared about my own texture, my students began to trust me and believe that I wanted the best for them.

While I do all of this, I also ensure that I maintain a level of professionalism. I've seen teachers blur, and at times, cross a line in the name of relationship building. Not only can that cause damage to students by modeling unhealthy boundaries, it also can be problematic when considering racial context. In some cases I've seen White teachers cross that line, resulting in saviorism when working with students who are people of color. Saviorism is when a teacher centers themselves and their efforts in a performative effort to save their students. This is often an unconscious or unintended effort, but it's saviorism nonetheless. It doesn't solve the larger issues at play and will only keep that student dependent on that teacher in a way that is condescending. It's a trope I've seen way too many times. So when we share ourselves with students in a healthy way, we set up a space that is conducive to relationship building and trust, not codependency or performance.

It's Time

I want to hug you with these words: we are in no position to consider ourselves apolitical or neutral members of society. As educators, we are either dismantling the unjust system that is education, or we are complicit in it. We were never neutral. We were never apolitical. And political doesn't mean partisan. It refers to elements of our identity that, in this country, have social implications on our quality of life. When we choose to teach only canonical texts or a strict classical education, or when we choose to not talk about racism, sexism, homophobia, or other isms with students, we are uplifting the project of Whiteness that has harmed us all for too long. And that is very political. Indeed, it has literally created the pathway for oppressive policies and politics. Know that when you teach in a holistic way that is working toward our liberation, you will receive pushback and you will face discomfort. When he spoke at the March on Washington, the late Representative John Lewis called on his constituents to get into "good trouble." I echo his imperative: to be on the right side of history, you need to get into "good trouble." To be clear, I'm not encouraging you to do something that will get you fired. You need to stay in a position to continue teaching for social justice. What I mean is to push strategically and consistently and as often as you can. You'll know if and when it becomes an environment you need to walk away from.

Fighting for justice and equity in education requires commitment and persistence.

When that woven fabric that my aunt was talking about is finished, it might look like an impossible feat or even magic. Beholders are left impressed by the way the colors and the patterns come together. They marvel at the weaver and are in awe of their work. It's important to know it's not magic, though. There isn't anything mysterious about how it all came together. It's a task that took time, patience, creativity, and dedication. It required commitment to see the work through. It necessitated a persistent individual. That is also the case for Textured Teaching. At the end of the unit or at the end of the year, onlookers might think you have a teaching spark or that you're special. And although you might both have a spark and be a beautifully special individual, it was also because you worked hard. You insisted on improving your craft and striving for a culturally sustaining pedagogy. Fighting for justice and equity in education requires commitment and persistence. It's time we get to work. It's always been our time.

REFERENCES

Acevedo, Elizabeth. 2018. *The Poet X*. New York: HarperCollins.

Adeyemi, Tomi. 2018. *Children of Blood and Bone*. New York: Henry Holt & Co.

Adichie, Chimamanda Ngozi. 2009. "The Danger of a Single Story." TEDGlobal. www.ted.com/talks/chimamanda_ngozi_adichie_the_danger_of_a_single_story?language=en.

Alvarez, Julia. 1995. *In the Time of the Butterflies*. New York: Plume.

———. 2009. *Return to Sender*. New York: Penguin Random House.

Anderson, Laurie H. 2000. *Fever 1793*. New York: Simon & Schuster Books for Young Readers.

Anzaldúa, Gloria. 1995. "Linguistic Terrorism." In *Latina: Women's Voices from the Borderlands*, edited by Lillia Castillo-Speed, 250–256. New York: Touchstone.

———. 2012. *Borderlands/La Frontera*. San Francisco: Aunt Lute.

Au, Wayne, Jesse Hagopian, and Dyan Watson. 2018. *Teaching for Black Lives*. Milwaukee, WI: Rethinking Schools.

Barroso, Mariano, dir. 2001. *In the Time of the Butterflies*. Film. Showtime Networks, released by Metro-Goldwyn-Mayer.

Berg, Jill Harrison. 2019. "Leading Together / Following the Lead of Teachers of Color." *Educational Leadership* 76 (7): 87–88. www.ascd.org/publications/educational-leadership/apr19/vol76/num07/Following-the-Lead-of-Teachers-of-Color.aspx.

Bishop, Marlon, and Tatiana Fernandez. 2017. "80 Years On, Dominicans and Haitians Revisit Painful Memories of Parsley Massacre." NPR. www.npr.org/sections/parallels/2017/10/07/555871670/80-years-on-dominicans-and-haitians-revisit-painful-memories-of-parsley-massacre.

Bomba Estéreo. 2017. "Soy Yo." *Amanecer*. Sony Music Entertainment.

Bratt, Peter, dir. 2018. *Delores*. Film. PBS. www.pbs.org/independentlens/films/dolores-huerta/.

Butler, Octavia E. 1979. *Kindred*. New York: Doubleday.

Calle 13. 2010. "Latinoamérica." *Entren Los Que Quieran*. Sony Music Latin.

Cardoso, Patricia, dir. 2002. *Real Women Have Curves.* Film. Newmarket Films.

Cisneros, Sandra. 1991. *The House on Mango Street.* New York: Vintage Books.

CNN Tonight. 2015. "If I Use the N-Word It Could Cost Me My Career." March 17. www.cnn.com/videos/us/2015/03/17/ctn-ben-ferguson-marc-lamont-hill -trinidad-james-n-word-debate-block-2.cnn.

Coates, Ta-Nehisi. 2015. *Between the World and Me.* New York: Speigel and Grau.

———. 2017. "Te-Nehisi Coates on Words That Don't Belong to Everyone." *We Were Eight Years In Power* Book Tour. www.vox.com/identities/2017/11/9/16627900 /ta-nehisi-coates-n-word.

Collins, Cory. 2018. "What Is White Privilege, Really? Recognizing White Privilege Begins with Truly Understanding the Term Itself." *Learning for Justice.* 60 (Fall).

Cornell, Joseph. *The Joseph Cornell Box* (blog). www.josephcornellbox.com.

Dabrowski, Joan, and Tanji Reed Marshall. 2018. "Motivation and Engagement in Student Assignments: The Role of Choice and Relevancy." The Education Trust. https://edtrust.org/resource/motivation-and-engagement-in-student -assignments/.

Danticat, Edwidge. 1995. *Krik? Krak!* Milano: Baldini & Castoldi.

DiAngelo, Robin. 2018. *White Fragility: Why It's So Hard for White People to Talk About Racism.* Boston: Beacon Press.

Dunbar-Ortiz, Roxanne. 2015. *An Indigenous Peoples' History of the United States.* Boston: Beacon Press.

———. 2019. *An Indigenous Peoples' History of the United States for Young People.* Adapted by Jean Mendoza and Debbie Reese. Boston: Beacon Press.

Ebarvia, Tricia. 2017. "How Inclusive Is Your Literacy Classroom Really?" *Heinemann Blog.* https://blog.heinemann.com/heinemann-fellow-tricia-ebavaria-inclusive -literacy-classroom-really.

Ewing, Eve L. 2019. *Ghosts in the Schoolyard: Racism and School Closings on Chicago's South Side.* Chicago: The University of Chicago Press.

Farmer, Nancy. 1994. *The Ear, the Eye and the Arm.* New York: Orchard Books.

Ferrera, America. 2016. "Thank You, Donald Trump!" www.huffpost.com/entry /thank-you-donald-trump_b_7709126.

———. 2019. "My Identity Is a Superpower—Not an Obstacle." TED Talk. www.ted.com/talks/america_ferrera_my_identity_is_a_superpower_not _an_obstacle?utm_campaign=social&utm_medium=referral&utm_source =t.co&utm_content=talk&utm_term=humanities.

Freire, Paulo. 2000. *Pedagogy of the Oppressed.* New York: Continuum.

Geda, Fabio. 2010. *In the Sea There Are Crocodiles.* New York: Anchor Books.

Goldstein, Phyllis. 2011. *A Convenient Hatred: The History of Antisemitism.* Brookline, MA: Facing History and Ourselves.

Gómez-Peña, Guillermo, Enrique Chagoya, and Felicia Rice. 2000. *Codex Espanglienses: From Columbus to the Border Patrol.* San Francisco: City Lights Books.

Gonzalez, Jennifer. 2015. "The Big List of Class Discussion Strategies." *Cult of Pedagogy* (blog). www.cultofpedagogy.com/speaking-listening-techniques/.

————. 2019. "Think Twice Before Doing Another Historical Simulation." *Cult of Pedagogy* (blog). www.cultofpedagogy.com/classroom-simulations/.

Greenwald, Noah, Brian Segee, Tierra Curry, and Curt Bradley. 2017. "A Wall in the Wild: The Disastrous Impacts of Trump's Border Wall on Wildlife." www.biologicaldiversity.org/programs/international/borderlands_and _boundary_waters/pdfs/A_Wall_in_the_Wild.pdf.

Guerra, Juan Luis. 1990. "Bachata Rosa." *Bachata Rosa.* Karen Music.

————. 1990. "Carta de Amor." *Bachata Rosa.* Karen Music.

Gyasi, Yaa. 2016. *Homegoing: A Novel.* New York: Vintage Books.

Hammond, Zaretta. 2014. *Culturally Responsive Teaching and the Brain.* Thousand Oaks, CA: Corwin.

Harvard T. H. Chan School of Public Health. 2018. "Discrimination in America: Final Summary." https://cdn1.sph.harvard.edu/wp-content/uploads/sites/94/2018/01 /NPR-RWJF-HSPH-Discrimination-Final-Summary.pdf.

Hill, Lauryn, 1998. "Everything Is Everything." *The Miseducation of Lauryn Hill.* Columbia Records.

Hill, Marc Lamont. 2009. *Beats, Rhymes, and Classroom Life.* New York: Teachers College Press.

hooks, bell. 1994. *Teaching to Transgress.* New York: Routledge.

Immortal Technique. 2005. "Bin Laden." Babygrande Records.

Irizarry, Jason. 2011. *The Latinization of U.S. Schools: Successful Teaching and Learning in Shifting Cultural Contexts.* Boulder, CO: Paradigm.

Jacobs, Harriet. 1861. *Incidents in the Life of a Slave Girl.* London: Thayer & Eldridge.

Jewell, Tiffany. 2020. *This Book Is Anti-Racist.* Minneapolis, MN: Quarto.

Johnson, Latrice P., and Maisha T. Winn. 2011. *Writing Instruction in the Culturally Relevant Classroom.* Urbana, IL: National Council of Teachers of English.

Jones, Kenneth, and Tema Okun. 2001. "White Supremacy Culture Characteristics."
   Showing Up for Racial Justice (blog). www.showingupforracialjustice
   .org/white-supremacy-culture-characteristics.html.

Kay, Matthew R. 2018. *Not Light, but Fire: How to Lead Meaningful Race Conversations in the Classroom.* United States: Portsmouth, NH: Stenhouse.

Kendi, Ibram X. 2019. *How to Be an Antiracist.* New York: One World.

Keys, Alicia. 2012. "Girl on Fire." *Girl on Fire.* RCA.

Khan, Nahnatchka. 2014. "Fresh Off the Boat Trailer." *Fresh Off the Boat.* ABC.

King, Jr., Martin Luther. 1963. *Strength to Love.* New York: Harper & Row.

Kinloch, Valerie. 2010. *Harlem on Our Minds: Place, Race, and the Literacies of Urban
   Youth.* New York: Teachers College Press.

Kirwan Institute for the Study of Race and Ethnicity. 2015. "Understanding Implicit
   Bias." The Ohio State University. https://kirwaninstitute.osu.edu/research
   /understanding-implicit-bias.

Kochiyama, Yuri. 2004. *Passing It On: A Memoir.* Los Angeles: UCLA Asian American
   Studies Center Press.

Ladson-Billings, Gloria. 1995. "Toward a Theory of Culturally Relevant Pedagogy."
   American Educational Research Journal 32 (3): 465–91. http://lmcreadinglist
   .pbworks.com/f/Ladson-Billings%20%281995%29.pdf.

Learning for Justice. 2017. "Let's Talk! Discussing Race, Racism and Other Difficult
   Topics with Students." www.learningforjustice.org/professional-development
   /webinars/lets-talk-discussing-race-racism-and-other-difficult-topics-0.

———. 2018. *Social Justice Standards: The Teaching Tolerance Anti-Bias Framework.*
   https://www.learningforjustice.org/frameworks/social-justice-standards.

———. 2019. "Hate at School." Montgomery, AL: Southern Poverty Law Center.

Lee, Spike, dir. 1989. *Do the Right Thing.* Universal Pictures.

Library of Congress. 2020. "Chinese Exclusion Act: Primary Documents in American
   History." https://guides.loc.gov/chinese-exclusion-act.

Lorca, Federico García. 1993. *Three Plays: Blood Wedding, Yerma, The House of
   Bernarda Alba.* New York: Farrar, Straus and Giroux.

McIntyre, Hugh. 2017. "Report: Hip-Hop/R&B Is the Dominant Genre in the US for the
   First Time." Forbes. www.forbes.com/sites/hughmcintyre/2017/07/17/hip-hoprb
   -has-now-become-the-dominant-genre-in-the-u-s-for-the-firstime
   /?sh=7f17d10a5383.

Medina, José. n.d. "The C6 Biliteracy Framework: Lesson Planning Through a Critical Consciousness Lens." ELLevation. https://ellevationeducation.com/blog /biliteracy-framework-lesson-planning.

Michon, Corey. 2016. "Uncovering Mass Incarceration's Literacy Disparity." *Prison Policy Initiative.* www.prisonpolicy.org/blog/2016/04/01/literacy/.

Morrison, Toni. 1992. *Playing in the Dark: Whiteness and the Literary Imagination.* New York: Vintage Books.

———. 1993. *The Bluest Eye.* New York: Knopf.

Muhammad, Gholdy. 2019. *Cultivating Genius.* New York: Scholastic.

Nas. 1996. "I Gave You Power." *It Was Written.* Columbia Records.

———. 2003. "I Can." *God's Son.* Columbia Records.

National Council of Teachers of English. 2019. "Statement on Independent Reading." https://ncte.org/statement/independent-reading/.

Nelson, Stanley, dir. 2016. *The Black Panthers: Vanguard of the Revolution.* Film. PBS. https://www.pbs.org/independentlens/films/the-black-panthers -vanguard-of-the-revolution/.

Newlevant, Hazel, and Desiree Rodriguez. 2018. *Puerto Rico Strong: A Comics Anthology Supporting Puerto Rico's Disaster.* St. Louis, MO: Lion Forge.

New York Times Magazine. 2019. "The 1619 Project." www.nytimes.com /interactive/2019/08/14/magazine/1619-america-slavery.html.

Okun, Tema. n.d."White Supremacy Culture." DRWorksBook. www.dismantlingracism.org/white-supremacy-culture.html.

Ortiz, Karla, and Francisca Ortiz. 2016. "Karla Ortiz & Francisca Ortiz on Immigration-Democratic National Convention." YouTube. www.youtube.com /watch?v=qJJpYBxrW9c.

Paris, Django, and Samy Alim, eds. 2017. *Culturally Sustaining Pedagogies: Teaching and Learning for Justice in a Changing World.* New York: Teachers College Press.

Pichardo-Espaillat, Tomas. n.d. "Ugly History: The 1937 Haitian Massacre." TedEd. https://ed.ted.com/lessons/ugly-history-the-1937-haitian-massacre -edward-paulino.

Price, Sean. 2011. "Straight Talk About the N-Word." www.learningforjustice.org /magazine/fall-2011/straight-talk-about-the-nword.

Public Enemy. 1989. "Fight the Power." Motown Records.

Quintero. Isabel. 2014. *Gabi, a Girl in Pieces*. El Paso, TX: Cinco Puntos.

Reese, Debbie. 2019. "Are You Planning to Do a Land Acknowledgement?" *American Indians in Children's Literature*. (blog). https://americanindiansinchildrens literature.blogspot.com/2019/03/are-you-planning-to-do-land.html.

Reynolds, Jason. 2016. *Ghost*. New York: Atheneum.

———. 2017. *Long Way Down*. New York: Atheneum.

Reynolds, Jason, and Ibram X. Kendi. 2020. *Stamped: Racism, Antiracism, and You*. Boston: Little, Brown Books for Young Readers.

Roberts, Deborah. www.DeborahRobertsArt.com.

Rodriguez, R. Joseph. 2019. *Teaching Culturally Sustaining and Inclusive Young Adult Literature: Critical Perspectives and Conversations*. New York: Routledge.

Satrapi, Marjane. 2004. *Persepolis: The Story of a Childhood*. San Francisco: Pantheon.

Serravallo, Jennifer. 2018. *Understanding Texts & Readers: Responsive Comprehension Instruction with Leveled Texts*. Portsmouth, NH: Heinemann.

Shakur, Assata. 1987. *Assata: An Autobiography*. Chicago: Chicago Review Press.

Shakur, Tupac. 1991. "Brenda's Got A Baby." *2Pacalypse Now*. Interscope Records.

———. 1993. "Keep Ya Head Up." *Strictly 4 My N.I.G.G.A.Z*. Interscope Records.

———. 1998. "Changes." *Greatest Hits*. Interscope Records.

———. 1999. *The Rose That Grew from Concrete*. New York: Pocket Books.

Shelley, Mary. 1818. *Frankenstein*. London: London Publishing House.

Sims Bishop, Rudine. 1990. "Mirrors, Windows, and Sliding Glass Doors." *Perspectives: Choosing and Using Books for the Classroom* 6 (3). https://scenicregional .org/wp-content/uploads/2017/08/Mirrors-Windows-and-Sliding-Glass -Doors.pdf.

Singleton, Glenn. 2014. *Courageous Conversations About Race: A Field Guide for Achieving Equity in Schools,* 2d ed. Thousand Oaks, CA: Corwin.

Smitherman, Geneva. 1995. "African American English: From the Hood to the Amen Corner." Keynote speech: Linguistic Diversity and Academic Writing Conference. http://writing.umn.edu/lrs/assets/pdf/speakerpubs/Smitherman.pdf.

Snoop Lion. 2013. "No Guns Allowed." *Reincarnated*. Berhane Sound System.

Spectra Diversity. 2017. "Brain Stuff: The Neuroscience Behind Implicit Bias." www.spectradiversity.com/2017/12/27/unconscious-bias/.

Starkey, Brando Simeo. 2017. "If You Truly Knew What the N-Word Meant to Our Ancestors, You'd NEVER Use It." https://theundefeated.com/features /if-you-truly-knew-what-the-n-word-meant-to-our-ancestors-youd-never-use-it/.

Stavans, Ilan. 2009. *Becoming Americans: Four Centuries of Immigrant Writing.* New York: The Library of America.

Steele, C. M., and J. Aronson. 1995. "Stereotype Threat and the Intellectual Test Performance of African Americans." *Journal of Personality and Social Psychology* 69 (5): 797–811.

Stevenson, Bryan. 2014. *Just Mercy.* New York: Penguin Random House.

Stop the Violence Movement. 1989. "Self-Destruction." Power Play Studios.

Tatum, Beverly Daniel. 2017. *Why Are All the Black Kids Sitting Together in the Cafeteria?* New York: Basic Books.

Thomas, Angie. 2017. *The Hate U Give.* New York: Balzer + Bray.

Thomas, Ebony Elizabeth. 2019. *The Dark Fantastic: Race and the Imagination from Harry Potter to the Hunger Games.* New York: New York University Press.

Torres, Julia. 2018. "Literary Canon-Boom!" *juliaetorres.blog* (blog). https://juliaetorres.blog/2018/04/14/literary-canon-boom/.

Tuck, Eve. 2009. "Suspending Damage: A Letter to Communities." *Harvard Educational Review* 79 (3): 409–27. https://pages.ucsd.edu/~rfrank/class_web /ES-114A/Week%204/TuckHEdR79-3.pdf.

Twain, Mark. 1998. *The Adventures of Huckleberry Finn.* New York: W. W. Norton.

Vancour, Vanessa. 2017. "I'm Mexican. Does That Change Your Assumptions About Me?" TEDx Talk. www.youtube.com/watch?v=sE4-req-Hes&list=PLqXLul-k_wVX xUHZUOo8rEvikgcQSzxpu&index=9.

Vilson, Jose Luis. 2014. *This Is Not a Test: A New Narrative on Race, Class, and Education.* Chicago: Haymarket Books.

Vox. 2016. "The Depressingly Long History of Yellowface in Hollywood." Digg, April 21. https://digg.com/video/yellowface-hollywood.

Waheed, Nayyirah. 2013. *Salt.* San Bernardino, CA: CreateSpace Independent Publishing.

Weisel, Elie. 1960. *Night.* New York: Hill and Wang.

Wiggins, Grant, and Jay McTighe. 2005. *Understanding by Design.* Alexandria, VA: ASCD.

Williams-Garcia, Rita. 2010. *One Crazy Summer.* New York: Amistad.

WOLA. n.d. "Migration Through Mexico: A Humanitarian Emergency." www.wola.org/maps/1602_border/full-screen.html.

Wong, David H. T. 2012. *Escape to Gold Mountain: A Graphic History of the Chinese in North America.* Vancouver, Canada: Arsenal Pulp Press.

Yang, Gene Luen. 2006. *American Born Chinese.* New York: Roaring Book Press.